The Fingerprint of God

RECENT SCIENTIFIC DISCOVERIES REVEAL THE
UNMISTAKABLE IDENTITY OF THE CREATOR
second edition, revised and updated

Hugh Ross

Promise Publishing Co.
Orange, California 92667

Cover Photo:
> spiral galaxy NGC 5236 ("Southern Pinwheel") in the
> constellation Hydra, courtesy of National Optical Astronomy
> Observatories

The Fingerprint of God
First Edition © 1989 by Reasons To Believe
Second Edition © 1991 by Reasons To Believe
Published by Promise Publishing Co.
Orange, California 92667

Printed in the United States of America

Scripture quotations unless otherwise noted are from the Holy Bible,
New International Version, Copyright © 1973, 1978, 1984 International
Bible Society. Used by permission of Zondervan Bible Publishers.

Ross, Hugh
> The Fingerprint of God

ISBN 0-939497-18-2

Contents

Preface

How can we know whether or not God exists? For the last few centuries most scientists have promoted an atheistic or agnostic reply. In the last decade, however, a set of remarkable discoveries about the universe have dramatically jolted their position. Have cosmologists been forced to acknowledge the existence of God? If so, how?

Historically, the question "How did the universe begin?" has evoked chauvinistic replies from opposing camps:

- Scientists have said that there may be an answer, but it only will come through a study of science.
- Theologians have said that there may be an answer, but it only will come through a study of theology.
- Philosophers have concluded that there is no answer. Existentialists go so far as to declare that the question itself is absurd.

To tell the story of how the question has been answered—independently and corroboratively, by *both* science *and* theology—is the purpose of this book.

Preface to the second edition

Revisions and updates have been made on more than half the pages of the original book. The most significant additions have been made to Chapters 9, 12, 13, and 15. Chapter 9 includes new data and discussion on the latest measurements of redshifts, of the cosmic background radiation, and of the density of the universe which now prove beyond any reasonable doubt that the universe began with some kind of hot big bang. These measurements have even helped researchers eliminate one class of big bang models (the standard models) in favor of another class (inflationary cold dark matter big bangs). Several newly discovered design characteristics for the universe and Earth are added to Chapter 12 along with some calculations of the degree of fine-tuning required by several other parameters. More biblical support for long creation days is given in Chapter 13, and further consideration of God's personal involvement in dealing with human suffering appears in Chapter 15.

Notes on mathematical terms

This book speaks of quantities ranging from the immensely large to the minutely small. Thus, on occasion, you will see the shorthand "powers of ten" notation. For example, 10^{11} denotes 100,000,000,000 (that is, 1 with 11 zeros after it, or one hundred billion), and 10^{-13} denotes .0000000000001 (that is, 1 with 12 zeros in front of it, or one ten trillionth).

Mathematical equations appear in chapter 5 only. They are included to amplify the way in which certain conclusions were derived. These equations may be skipped over without destroying your grasp of the message of the book.

Acknowledgments

First and foremost I thank Kathy, my wife, whose many sacrifices gave me time to research and to write. Also, she acted as "editor-in-chief," pouring hundreds of hours into editing and rewriting. Her steadfast support in the midst of stress was a source of great encouragement to me.

Second, I thank those who gave of their time to work in our office and in our home in order to set Kathy and me free to concentrate on the book. Prominent among them are Patty Bradbury, Janice Finney, Gloria Kuo, Roberta Loutsenhizer, Lori Ozuna, Barbara Schwind, and Mara Weber.

Third, I thank the dozens of scholars, students, and audience participants who provided review, critique, and recommendations. I especially thank Drs. Don Page and Allan Sandage, also Steve Scheele and Davis Weyerhaeuser for theirs.

Fourth, I thank Mal Scharer and Drs. Walter Bradley, Michael Denton, John Patterson, and Allan Sandage for helping me find relevant research papers. Marj Harman I thank for her efforts in tracking down photographs.

Fifth, I thank Dr. David Carta, Dr. Samuel Conner, and Gordon Peterson for their many helpful suggestions for the second edition. I am grateful to Chuck Missler, Rich Buhler, Dr. James Dobson, and others for encouraging broadcast audiences to read this book and pass it along.

Finally, I thank Ed and Mary Belle Steele of Promise Publishing; my pastor, Richard Anderson; my church family, Sierra Madre Congregational; and the many friends who strongly urged me to devote the necessary time to write. Thanks also to the Reasons To Believe prayer team, who faithfully upheld this project to its completion, and who uphold it still.

PART ONE

Roots of Cosmology

In man's earliest attempts to explain origins lie the rudimentary tenets—and controversies—of modern studies in cosmology. Here these roots are traced and documented.

CHAPTER ONE

The Odd Couple

summary

Scientists and theologians are feuding over cosmology. At issue are the size, age, and design characteristics of the universe. The current animosity has deep roots.

fundamental issues

Cosmology is the study of the universe as a whole—its structure, origin, and development. The questions cosmology addresses are profound, both scientifically and theologically. Is the universe finite or infinite in content and extent? Is it eternal, or does it have a beginning? Was it created? If not, how did it get here? If so, how was this creation accomplished, and what can we learn about the agent and events of creation? Who or what governs the laws and constants of physics? Are they products of chance, or have they been designed? How do they relate to the support and development of life? Is there any existence, knowable existence, beyond the known dimensions of the universe? Is the universe running down, irreversibly, or will it bounce back?

A major, if not *the* major, bone of contention in cosmology has to do with origins—is a supreme being (God) responsible for the universe we observe or are random processes responsible for it? If the material and energy in the universe are infinite in quantity and in time, then under the right physical conditions an infinite variety of random processes might conceivably explain the appearance of even highly ordered and complex life forms. Similarly, if the ranges of the various conditions and characteristics required to bring about life in our universe are sufficiently broad, no need might exist for a personal creative agent. On the other hand, if the matter and energy are finite in extent and in time, and if the ranges of the parameters for life are narrow, we have potent evidence for a personal Creator, specifically for the God of the Bible.[a] Thus, size, age, and design figure critically in the debate over who or what is behind the universe.

scientists' response

These factors now are open to close investigation by astronomers and physicists. As new instruments penetrate deeply into the origins and outwardly to the limits of the universe, physicists and astronomers have been tempted to think that science has, or ultimately will have, all the answers, "naturalistic" answers to the questions surrounding origins. Many react against any attempts to draw theistic inferences from their findings. In his 1931 presidential address to the Mathematical Association of Great Britain, Sir Arthur Eddington proposed, "Some people would like to call this non-random feature of the world purpose or design; but I will call it non-committally anti-chance."[1] Writing in 1948, Sir Fred Hoyle declared, "It is against the spirit of scientific enquiry to regard observable effects as arising from 'causes unknown to science.'"[2] In the 1980 s, Paul Davies claims, "It is now possible to conceive of a scientific explanation for all creation." He argues the question, "Has modern physics abolished God altogether?" His answer (at least for the moment)—"It has!"[3]

---

a. In other words, a finite universe (or at least one significantly short of infinity) would rule out any atheistic or agnostic interpretation of origins. An infinite universe could be interpreted from either a theistic or a non-theistic perspective since God would have the freedom to create the universe infinite or finite. But, as chapter 12 presents, the laws of physics, the measured characteristics of the universe, and the restrictive realities of life support require that the universe be significantly finite.

theologians' response

On their part, theologians have been no less adamant in their presumption that science has no bearing on cosmological questions. The late Herman Bavinck, eminent theology professor of the Free University of Amsterdam, concluded that "this question of the origin of things lies outside of the domain of natural science."[4] He concurred with German philosopher Ernst Haeckel whom he quoted in saying, "If creation ever took place, 'it lies entirely beyond the scope of human knowledge, and hence can never become the object of scientific investigation.'"[4] In this one-sided perspective lie the roots of *single revelational theology* espoused by many conservative theologians today. According to one spokesman for this viewpoint, John C. Whitcomb, "Cosmogony, cosmology, and metaphysics ... must grope in darkness apart from God's special revelation in scripture."[5] Further, he asserts that "Christians must abandon all hope of formulating a scientifically valid cosmogony if they fall prey to the popular notion that science provides an independent and equally authoritative source of information with the Bible concerning the creation of the universe, the solar system, and the earth with its living forms; and that science alone is competent to tell us when and how such things occurred."[6]

sources of animosity

How sad it is that when theologians and scientists cross paths today, dialogue so often degenerates into name calling. Russell Akridge, speaking at the 1982 Annual Creation Convention, berates astrophysicists and astronomers as "high priests of the decades-old cult" of the "Big Bang myth," and as "persuasive speakers [who] have deceived an unsuspecting public."[7] Michael Ruse, professor of the history and philosophy of biology, on the other side, stingingly rails, "There are degrees of being wrong. The Creationists are at the bottom of the scale.

They pull every trick in the book to justify their position. Indeed, at times, they verge right over into the downright dishonest ... Their arguments are rotten, through and through."8 Such statements come from professionals who pride themselves in their objectivity and dispassion.

Obviously, when it comes to cosmology, and specifically to questions about origins, bitter animosity divides scientists and theologians. How did this hostility develop? Where there is ignorance, there is fear and anger. In spite of all their education, scientists and theologians are woefully uninformed of each other's disciplines. Few if any seminaries encourage, let alone require, their students to study modern science. Secular universities, for their part, have long since dropped theology from their science curriculum. At any rate, theologians tend to obtain their information about the universe indirectly through "science reading," while scientists tend to obtain their information about God and the Bible indirectly through "theology reading." Inevitably, interpretations are compared with facts rather than facts with facts. Polarization is the predictable result (see Table 1.1).

Table 1.1: Reasons why scientists and theologians are polarized
These generalizations, though sweeping, may help to describe the perspectives of today's scientists and theologians. In these contrasting world views lie many of the root causes for existing animosities.

scientists tend to	**theologians** tend to
have a natural outlook	have a supernatural outlook
rely on observations	rely on revelation
glorify human reasoning	glorify "faith"
use scientific methods	use exegetical methods
believe in a self-created universe	believe in a transcendent Creator
adjust theories by observational tests	adjust theories by absolute doctrines
see only science as objective	see only theology as objective

6

A final manifestation of this ignorance is a failure by many scientists and theologians to consider the historical roots of conflicts over cosmology. Thus, many simple misunderstandings have been perpetuated and needlessly debated. That is why our first step will be to look backward and to explore briefly the history of cosmology.

Before embarking on a historical sojourn, however, we need to acknowledge that the number of possible approaches to cosmology exceeds those discussed here. In between the atheistic and theistic world views are deism (belief that God created the universe and its natural laws, but takes no further part in its functioning), also agnosticism (belief that the human mind cannot know whether there is a God, an ultimate cause, or anything beyond material phenomena), and other philosophical perspectives almost as numerous as the individuals who address the subject of origins. Of necessity, any approach to cosmology involves science, philosophy, and theology—all three—with varying emphases.

CHAPTER TWO

Early Historical Roots

summary

The earliest cosmologies were thoroughly theological and non-scientific.   Later cosmologies originating from India left God (or gods) out.   Surprisingly, two of these primitive atheistic theories framed the modern steady state and oscillating universe cosmologies.   Later still, Roman philosopher Lucretius, through circular reasoning, eternalized matter and discarded the agency of divine creation.   Augustine, Maimonides, and Aquinas strongly attacked atheism, but often with faulty or misconstrued arguments from the Bible.

No conflict between scientists and theologians existed in ancient times because there were no scientists, at least not in the modern sense of the word.   With only 6000 stars visible and no tools for measurement (see Figure 2.1), ancient cosmologists tended to rely heavily on imagination and sentiment for their hypotheses.

oldest recorded cosmologies

Cosmology has always captured man's imagination. Man's oldest writings have cosmology as their theme. Some five to six thousand years ago, the Chinese, Egyptians, and Mesopotamians recorded their well developed cosmological myths.

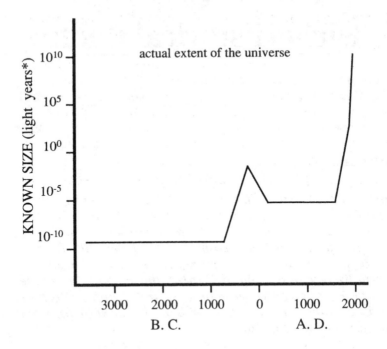

Figure 2.1: Man's awareness of the extent of the universe throughout recorded history

The scale is logarithmic. One unit on the vertical axis represents a 100,000-fold increase in the measured size of the universe. Note that for 1900 years (300 B.C. - 1600 A.D.) no progress was made in extending what was known of the limits of the universe, while in just 64 years (1923 - 1987) the known limits advanced from .001 percent to full measurement of the entire universe.

*One light year is equivalent to 5.9 trillion miles or 9.5 trillion kilometers.

The Chinese viewed the earth as a square with China at the center, the heavens as a canopy of stars split into four quarters and centered on the polestar. The sun and moon were gods that could be combined with any single concept to form an "all embracing, uniquely eternal, creative wholeness."

In Egypt, the earth was considered the rectangular foundation for the universe. A goddess, resting her feet and hands on the four corners of the earth, arched her starry body over the earth while permitting the Sun and Moon deities to glide daily over her legs, back, and arms. The Milky Way was said to be the celestial twin god of the Nile. Along it the planets (all deities in their own right) allegedly sailed their boats. These deities were assigned responsibility for creating everything else.

The Mesopotamians described the earth as a floating vessel on the "waters of the deep." Above it stood a solid dome, covered with the "waters above," which occasionally seeped through—rain. The sun, moon, and stars whirled around on the inner surface of the dome. These heavenly lights were thought to be eternal deities, creators of the material elements of the universe—water, earth, sky (that is, the dome), and possibly fire.

Virtually all ancient cosmologists conceived of the physical universe as finite in extent and in age. Existence beyond the physical universe was accepted by all. One (or more) of the deities or creative agents was credited with bringing into existence physical matter, plants, animals, and human beings.

first atheistic hypothesis

India's cosmologists in the centuries that followed formed a distinctly contrasting view of the universe. To be sure, gods did exist in their various philosophical systems, but these gods were said to originate *after* the formation of the universe or to play no part in forming the universe, which arose, rather, from some nonpersonal spirit or power. According to the majority of these Indian cosmologists, the universe proceeded through an infinite number of cycles. At the end of each cycle every particle "dissolved into the primal, pure waters of eternity" from which everything once again emerged, phoenix-like, from its own ashes. Scientists or not, these ancient theorists

11

preempted the modern proponents of the oscillating theory (see chapter 10), even to the setting of the period of the cycles at several billions of years.[1,2]

Two other schools of Indian cosmology, the Jains and the Mimamsa, held the universe to be eternal and changeless. The modern steady state theory (see chapter 8) thus was predated, at least in concept, by two or three millennia.

cultural universals

China, Egypt, Mesopotamia, and India were not alone in spawning cosmological hypotheses. Virtually every culture generated its own account of the origin of the universe.[3-6] Clearly, the question of ultimate origins proves irresistibly intriguing to mankind.

Greek observational cosmology

The first significant scientific efforts to determine the structure of the universe were made by the ancient Greeks. Ionian astronomer Thales in the seventh century B.C. noted that while the Big Dipper constellation never dropped below the horizon in Greece, it did in Egypt. His pupil (according to tradition), Anaximander, concluded that the earth could not be flat, but must be a sphere floating free within a sky of stars, itself spherical in shape.

Born late in the fourth century B.C., Aristarchus actually calculated (relative to the earth's diameter) the distances from earth and the sizes of the sun and the moon. He did this through geometric measurements of the moon's phases and of the size of the earth's shadow relative to the moon's diameter during a lunar eclipse.[7,a]

---

a. At exactly the first and third quarters of the moon's phases, the angles earth-moon-sun are 90 degrees. Measuring the angles sun-earth-moon at these times permits the geometric solution of the triangles. When the moon is partially eclipsed by the earth's shadow, the curved shape of the shadow yields the earth's diameter relative to the moon's.

Though his measurements for the sun were twenty times too small, they still revealed the sun to be enormously larger than the earth. In fact, the size difference was so great that Aristarchus concluded that the sun, not the earth, occupied the center of the universe.

Aristarchus also determined that the stars must be at least many millions of miles away. He based this determination on his total inability to observe parallaxes[b] for any of the stars. In short, Aristarchus established a remarkably accurate picture of the solar system, and of the system of visible stars, some two thousand years ahead of Copernicus.

Eratosthenes in the third century B.C. converted Aristarchus' relative distances and diameters into actual length measurements by determining the earth's diameter.[c] This he accomplished by measuring the angle of sunlight at locations of known distances apart.[8, 9]

These new measurements convinced most Greek scholars that the universe reflected divine design. The order and harmony they observed everywhere in the universe, extending even to the million-fold increase in what they had known of its size, confirmed to them its supernatural creation.

---

b. Parallax is the apparent change in the position of an object relative to much more distant objects due to the motion of an observer. For example, as an observer allows the earth in its orbit about the sun to move him some 180 million miles, he will be able to detect with the aid of a medium-sized telescope what seems to be a slight change in position for a nearby star relative to much more distant stars.

c. Eratosthenes knew the sun to be distant enough that its light rays would fall along roughly parallel lines at the earth. Therefore, the angle between the sun and the zenith at Alexandria (in northern Egypt) would equal the angle between Alexandria and Syene (in southern Egypt) at the earth's center. Thus, having measured the distance between Alexandria and Syene as 5000 stadia, Eratosthenes calculated the earth's circumference as $(360 \times 5000) \div (\sim 7° \times \pi)$ stadia.

Plato, Aristotle

A new mood in philosophy began to undermine the scientific base for research in cosmology. The philosophy of Plato (4th century B.C.) and others disdained the visible world and exalted the "real" world of ideas and abstractions. Experimental science was considered by Plato and his disciples to be "mere engineering"—not worth the attention of great intellects. Plato wrote in the *Republic:*

> It is by means of problems, then, said I, as in the study of geometry, that we will pursue astronomy too, and we will let be the things in the heavens, if we are to have a part in the true science of astronomy.[10]

Aristotle, one of Plato's students, philosophized that any past motion of the earth must naturally be towards the center of the universe. Therefore, he said, it is clear that the earth does not move.

church dogma

In subsequent generations the Orthodox and Roman Catholic churches sought to impose their authority over the entire western world. In order to engender unquestioning subservience to their clergy, these churches taught that "knowledge proceeds from rational conviction," that "faith precedes knowledge,"[11, d] and that this conviction and faith are dispensed through the sole agency of the clergy. Recognizing the similarity of these ideas to Aristotle's scholastic elitism and contempt for experimental science, the Orthodox and especially the Roman Catholic churches found it expedient to encourage the canonizing of Aristotle's philosophical pronouncements as inviolable dogma.

---

d. Ironically, the definition for *faith* that these churches chose stands in contradiction to the Bible. According to the Bible, faith is founded on fact and on what God has clearly done. See Isaiah 50:10 and Hebrews 11:1, also examples in Exodus 4:5, 19:9; Isaiah 41:20, 43:9-10, John 11:15, 11:42, 13:19, 14:29, 19:35, and 20:31.

Thus, the scientific (but not the theistic) cosmological foundations laid by the Greek observational astronomers were almost completely erased. Cosmological discussions had by this time evolved through three stages:

1. *scientific theism* founded by the Greek observational astronomers,

2. *philosophical theism* founded by Plato and Aristotle, and

3. *dogmatic theism* founded by Orthodox and Roman Catholic theologians.

Revolts against theistic cosmology, though rare, did occur, however, and these gave rise to vigorous debate.

Lucretius

Lucretius, a Roman in the first century B.C., chose (for reasons we can only guess) to swim against the strong tide of theistic creationism and to contend for an atheistic cosmology. But, he began with a theological assumption that begged the question, "Our starting-point will be this principle: Nothing can ever be created by divine power out of nothing."[12] He sought to prove his assumption through an observation about nature: "For if things came to being from nothing, every kind might be born from all things; nought would need a seed."[13]

Subsequently, Lucretius adopted from Democritus (4th century B.C. Greek philosopher) the concept of "atoms" as the fundamental, eternal components of all matter. Rather than theorizing just an infinite number of universes, he postulated an infinite number of universes going through unending cycles of formation, dissolution, and reformation. He acknowledged that the random assembly of atoms would not always form a well ordered life-bearing world, but reasoned that an infinite number of cycles in an infinite number of universes would overcome the improbability. He did concede, however, the need for a mechanism to guarantee the longevity of a cycle.[13, 14]

The modern "molecules to man" hypothesis, now routinely taught in the biological sciences,[15] has its roots in the ideas of Lucretius. According to modern proponents of Lucretian philosophy, life, though enormously improbable through chance processes, occurs because of the infinite number of opportunities available. However, unlike many modern materialists, Lucretius did acknowledge that it is not enough to form life; life must be made to last.

Lucretius had little influence on his contemporaries except perhaps on Virgil. Five centuries later, however, atheists revived altered forms of his cosmology. It was against this revival that Roman Catholic scholars, led by Augustine, launched an all-out attack.

Augustine's errors and contributions

Augustine (354 - 430 A.D.) properly noted that the Bible makes extensive use of cosmological arguments to prove God's existence. But, from this he presumed that the Bible could be and should be used to defeat any and all ideas proposed by atheists. Since some atheists were proposing "antipodes," or people on the opposite side of the globe, "who walk with their feet [diametrically] opposite ours," Augustine denounced the theory as "on no grounds credible."[16] He primarily objected to their assumption about the roundness of the earth, which he thought to be disproved by Bible verses such as Psalm 104:2, where the writer says that God "stretchest out the heavens like a curtain."

Incredibly, Augustine's refutation held. No one questioned Augustine's misinterpretation of the Hebrew word for curtain, yerî'â, which literally refers to a tent—walls and ceilings—not just to a two-dimensional "curtain." Nearly everyone had forgotten or ignored the work of Anaximander, Aristarchus, and Eratosthenes. Forgotten, too, were Bible verses such as Isaiah 40:22 that explicitly describe the sphericity of the earth.

Not content to have merely silenced the opposition on this one point, Augustine proceeded to develop five "irrefutable" proofs of God's existence:[e]

1. *the cosmological argument*—the effect of the universe's existence must have a suitable cause.

2. *the teleological argument*—the design of the universe implies a purpose or direction behind it.

3. *the rational argument*—the operation of the universe according to order and natural law implies a mind behind it.

4. *the ontological argument*—man's ideas of God, his God-consciousness, implies a God who imprinted such a consciousness.

5. *the moral argument*—man's built-in sense of right and wrong can be accounted for only by innate awareness of a code of law, awareness implanted by a higher being.

Unfortunately, this tour de force served to complicate unnecessarily the case for God's existence.

Maimonides

In the twelfth century, Jewish philosopher Moses Maimonides, in *Guide for the Perplexed,* sought to establish God's existence through proofs for a "primary mover," a "primary cause," a "necessary being." His starting point was that motion requires a cause. Reasoning that the series of its causes cannot be infinite, he concluded that there must be a first cause, hence a being to initiate motion.[17]

Having reasoned, thus, for God's existence, Maimonides attacked Aristotle's and Plato's doctrines of

---

e. These proofs, compiled and summarized by later generations of Roman Catholic scholars, were discussed at great length in Augustine's *Confessions, City of God,* and *On the Free Choice of the Will.* These works may be found in *Great Books of the Western World, volume 18, Augustine,* edited by Robert Maynard Hutchins (Chicago: Encyclopædia Britannica, 1952).

the eternity of the universe. He argued that an eternal universe contradicts the biblically-stated free operation of God's will. To his thinking, irregularities of planetary motion provided extra-biblical proof of God's free operation.

Aquinas

In the thirteenth century Thomas Aquinas, building on Maimonides' proofs for God's existence, extended and subdivided Augustine's cosmological argument:

a. Where there is motion, there is a mover, and ultimately a first mover, itself unmoved.

b. Things here are produced by their causes; these causes in turn were produced by their causes, and so on. Ultimately, there must be a first cause which is itself uncaused.

c. Contingent things demand as their ultimate explanation a non-contingent being.

d. Where there are degrees of perfection, there must ultimately be absolute perfection.

e. There are design and government in the world. Hence there are ultimately a first designer and a first governor.[18, 19]

The philosophical and theological arguments of Augustine, Maimonides, and Aquinas, despite serious weaknesses, were sufficient, given the support of the Roman Catholic hegemony, to guarantee the dominance in cosmology of theistic creation for centuries. In fact, the European scientific community, such as it was, tended to interpret all research findings from an Augustinian and/or Aquinian viewpoint. Inadvertently, however, by subdividing the Bible's cosmological argument into three parts (cosmological, teleological, and rational) and later into seven, Augustine and Aquinas opened the way for later piecemeal attacks on their "proofs."

CHAPTER THREE

Rebirth of Science

summary

The invention of movable type inaugurated a learning explosion that the Roman Catholic and Orthodox churches were unable to suppress. With new mathematics, Kepler and Newton used the copious observations of Tycho to establish a scale for the universe much vaster than any previously imagined. In spite of his strong theistic beliefs, Newton concluded that his laws of motion required an infinite universe. Neither the astronomers nor the theologians of the time were yet aware that Newton's laws and other basic laws of physics collided head-on with Archbishop Ussher's chronology of the Bible.

The anti-science mood triggered by Plato and encouraged by the Roman Catholic and Orthodox churches was so stifling that no significant astronomical investigations were made in Europe until after the middle ages. Outside Europe, Muslims were the most advanced in astronomy but contented themselves with those studies that would give them the direction to Mecca, the times for prayer, and a predictable calendar. By the thirteenth century, however, Muslim scholars had exported to Europe the new mathematics from India, including trigonometry, algebra, and the counting of numerals from zero.

cosmological recovery

After Gutenberg's invention of movable type in 1456, 40,000 printed works were published within a single generation.[1] This sudden availability of information generated an explosion of learning that has been sustained to this day.

One of the earliest beneficiaries of the publication boom was Nicolas Copernicus. From 1491-1506 he studied in Cracow, Bologna, Rome, Padua, and Ferrare, where the world's greatest libraries could be found. Upon reading Ptolemy, he surmised that it would be unworthy of the Creator to need so many circles to move the sun, moon, and planets around the earth. Copernicus then picked up the works of the ancient Greeks and Romans, discovering their heliocentric theories and their measurements of vast distance to the stars. Their ideas made sense to him. He studied diligently and produced a book, *De Revolutionibus,* published posthumously. In it Copernicus not only revived the heliocentric theory but, in referring geocentric observations of the planets to a heliocentric coordinate system, showed that the nearer a planet to the sun, the greater its orbital velocity. He thereby worked out the correct scale for the solar system.

reaction of religious leaders

The Roman Catholic curia interpreted heliocentrism as a direct assault on its doctrines. Therefore, when Galileo, the Renaissance father of experimental science, produced several observational evidences for the heliocentric theory,[2, 3] he established himself as an enemy of the Church. What piqued the prelates most was that Galileo, a mere layman, dared to call into question their pronouncements on biblical interpretation. In a letter to the Benedictine monk, Benedetto Castelli, Galileo said,

> The holy scriptures cannot err and the decrees therein contained are absolutely true and inviolable. But ... its expounders and interpreters are liable to err in many ways;

and one error in particular would be most grave and frequent, if we always stopped short at the literal signification of the words.[4]

The scriptures in question were Psalms 93:1 and 104:5 and Ecclesiastes 1:4-5, all of which seem to express the immovability of the earth. Galileo pointed out that regardless of how the earth moves, an earth-bound frame of reference by definition always generates an immovable earth. (If the earth is moving at velocity v relative say to the sun, then its movement relative to itself is $v - v = 0$.) Galileo noted that all three Bible passages speak from an earth-bound point of view. Galileo was emphasizing how essential it is to establish the frame of reference when conducting any scientific or exegetical inquiry.

The generation following Galileo understood intellectually the resolution of this conflict. However, emotional resolution came much more slowly. Galileo's published works on heliocentrism remained on the Church's Index of Prohibited Books until 1835, and not until 1981 did the Roman Catholic church officially forgive Galileo. Scientists' forgiveness of the church has been just as slow, if not slower, in coming. Some scientists report that past mistreatment of Galileo by the Roman Catholic church still stirs their indignation towards Christian churches and theologians, in general.

cosmological advance

Observational astronomy was reborn through Tycho Brahe (1546-1601), who devoted his entire adult life to making precise measurements of the positions of stars and planets. In the last year of his work, Tycho challenged his assistant, Johannes Kepler, to solve the problem of planetary motion. Using Tycho's copious data, Kepler derived three laws of planetary motion (published between 1609 and 1619) which enabled Isaac Newton to formulate his laws of motion and of universal gravitation (1687). Subsequent observations of stellar systems substantiated the pervasive validity of Newton's laws and indicated a size for the universe much vaster than any imagined by the ancient astronomers.

seeds of discord

The cosmological pioneers of the scientific revolution (Copernicus, Galileo, Tycho, Kepler, Newton, and others) were all devout men. To them, it was clear that God not only created the universe, but also had continually maintained its order and harmony. In fact, the scientific and theological communities were so at peace by the middle of the 17th century (at least in Protestant circles) that it was common for men to hold dual appointments in both astronomy and theology. However, it was during this period of amity that seeds of a future breach were sown.

One such seed was Newton's suggestion of an infinite universe. He noted in his theory of gravitation that every particle in the universe has an innate attraction toward all the rest. Hence, in a finite universe the matter at the outside edges would fall towards the matter inside. His proposal for a way out of this gravitational collapse was to suggest that matter is evenly distributed throughout an infinite space, a hypothesis which he thought would remove both the edges and the center of the universe.[5]

A second seed was planted by Cambridge University scholar John Lightfoot and by James Ussher, the Anglican archbishop of Ireland. In 1642, just 31 years after publication of the King James translation of the Bible, John Lightfoot authoritatively proclaimed September 17, 3928 B.C., as the date of the creation. A few years later Archbishop Ussher adjusted Lightfoot's date to October 3, 4004 B.C., and proceeded to derive specific dates for every historical event in the Bible.[6] Both Ussher and Lightfoot unfortunately assumed that 1) no generations were omitted from the biblical genealogies, and 2) the numbered days of the Genesis creation account were consecutive 24-hour days.

Soon, new editions of the King James translation incorporated Ussher's chronology as margin notes or even as headings. Many readers had difficulty distinguishing the commentator's chronology from the text. Further, the King James translation very quickly became *the* translation for the English-speaking world, and that world became the chief proponent of Protestantism. This intertwining of dates and text—and the fact that no serious objections to the dates were raised for over 150 years—helps us to understand why Ussher's time frame tended to become canonized in the minds of serious, practicing Protestants.

Even as early as the 17th century, alarms should have been sounded. Attempts to spread the Christian gospel in China were stymied because the Chinese historical records predated Ussher's chronology for the origin of human civilization.[6] Unfortunately, this problem stirred little notice in Europe or the Americas.

Gradually, through the developing field of celestial mechanics, came the recognition that Newton's laws of motion required minimum ages for stellar systems much in excess of Ussher's age for the universe. Though Newton himself had the mathematical means to deduce these minimum ages for stellar systems[a] (specifically, the relaxation times for such systems), the calculations were so tedious and the astronomical data so poor that more than two hundred years passed before formal calculations were attempted. Those calculations revealed to astronomers that Newton's law contradicted Ussher's chronology by at least a factor of a hundred thousand (see Figure 3.1).

---

a. For bodies far enough apart to behave as point sources (e.g. stars within star clusters), Carl Jacobi and Joseph Lagrange proved that Newton's laws of motion predict the positions and velocities of the bodies at any desired time, whether past or future, from a specified initial state.[7, 8] Given that all the stars in a cluster formed at about the same time (this can be confirmed by direct measurements), one can calculate the relaxation time, the time required for enough stellar encounters to occur so that the velocities of the stars are randomized towards statistical equilibrium.[9] Thus, if the measured stellar velocities reveal that statistical equilibrium has been achieved, then one has a minimum age for the cluster.

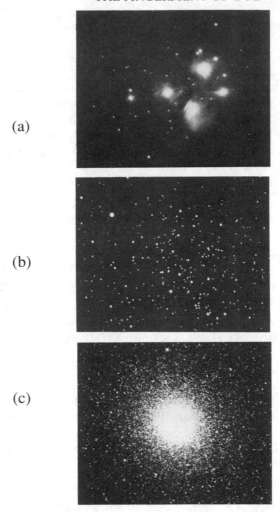

Figure 3.1: The star clusters, the Pleiades, M 67, and 47 Tuc

The relaxation time (see footnote *a*) for the stars in (a) the Pleiades is 20 million years, ten times greater for (b) M 67, and a hundred times greater for (c) 47 Tuc. One can imagine initial conditions so extreme as to reduce these ages considerably. Still, we are left with a contradiction of Ussher's chronology that cannot be overcome without a denial of the law of gravity and Newton's laws of motion.

Such calculations could conceivably be challenged by hypothesizing that much more extreme relaxation conditions predominated in the formative stages of stellar systems. However, a lower limit does exist. This limit would be the free fall time from the larger volume of the system at the formative stages to the much smaller volume of the system at the present time. This phenomenon, too, would be governed by Newton's laws (*free fall time* = 1/*gravitational constant* x *system density*). The free fall time for a galaxy would be about a billion years, for open star clusters, at least a million years, and for globular star clusters, about a hundred thousand years.

An even greater discrepancy between science and Ussher's timetable has developed with discoveries about stellar aging. Based simply on Newton's laws, gas laws, and the processes of nuclear fusion, astronomers can accurately predict the luminosity and effective temperature of any star (of any given mass) as a function of the star's age.[10, 11] Since the mass, luminosity, and effective temperature for a great many stars can be measured, astronomers possess a tool for reliably determining stellar ages. This tool indicates that there are stars 2,000,000 times older than Ussher's date for the creation. To dispute these stellar ages would mean rejecting basic hydrostatics, the thermodynamic gas laws, and nuclear transmutation.

Before the full impact of these disparities between Ussher's chronology and basic physics could be felt, however, the Protestant community had already split into two camps: conservative (those holding the Bible to be an error free book in all disciplines of study) and liberal (those viewing the Bible as requiring scholastic criticism to sift out the truth of God from human myth and error). The vast majority of scientists either joined the liberal camp or left the church altogether to follow the scientific agnosticism of Immanuel Kant (the subject of the next chapter). The end result? An inevitable polarization and alienation between conservative Protestants and the astronomers and other physical scientists.

CHAPTER FOUR

Rise of Non-Theism

summary

*Using Newton's laws, Kant proposed a strictly mech-
anistic model for the evolution of the universe. Buoyed by
favorable response to his supposed achievement, he
proceeded to knock down, through circular reasoning,
Augustine's and Aquinas' "irrefutable" arguments for
God's existence. Returning to his cosmological model, he
concluded that the universe must be infinite in both time
and space. From the time of Kant onward, the growing
mathematical complexity of astronomy chased more and
more theologians out of cosmology, leaving the theorizing
to Kant-influenced scientists. Furthermore, the phenomenal advances of observational astronomy seemed to support
Kant's hypothesis of an infinite universe. Kant's ideas not
only began to dominate cosmology and impact theology,
but they shaped the thinking that spawned many of the
"isms" of the nineteenth and twentieth centuries.*

Though speculations on an infinite universe had been
proffered by Giordano Bruno[1] and Thomas Digges[2] in the
late sixteenth century, not until 1734 was theistic
cosmology seriously challenged in the West. In that year
Swedish mystic Emanuel Swedenborg published his
explanation of the universe as the product of strictly
mechanistic evolution.[3] He theorized a means whereby
the stars would organize themselves into a vast rotating
system.

A few years later (in 1750) Thomas Wright deduced that the Milky Way must be a gigantic, lens-shaped, organized system of stars.[4] Cleverly combining the hypotheses of Swedenborg[a] and Wright, Immanuel Kant (in 1755, and more forcefully in 1781) delivered a coup d'état to the cosmologies, philosophies, and theologies of his day; in fact, of the preceding thirteen centuries.

Kant's cosmology

In his *Universal Natural History and Theory of the Heavens* (1755), Kant noted that the form of the Milky Way is similar to that of the solar system. Building upon James Bradley's and de la Hire's observational evidence that the stars do indeed "move,"[b] Kant conjectured that all the stars revolve in elliptical orbits, à la Newtonian mechanics, about the center of the Milky Way. Furthermore, since the best telescopes were beginning to detect among the stars nebulous spots roughly oval in shape, Kant presumed these to be distant star systems or "island universes" like the Milky Way, and proposed that all these heavenly systems emerged from a "primal nebula."

Kant's primal nebula is simply an aggregate of molecules in random motion. Kant surmised that from collisions of these molecules, small cores of mass would arise that would then attract other molecules. In this manner the primal nebula would condense into smaller nebulae, and, in turn, protostars would condense out of these nebulae. Nebular cloud remnants surrounding a protostar would begin rotating, according to Kant, as a result of successive impacts from collisions. Under the

a. Kant revealed his indebtedness to Swedenborg in his *Dreams of a Spirit-Seer Illustrated by the Dreams of Metaphysic*, published in 1766.
b. Ironically, Kant interpreted Bradley's discovery of the aberration of starlight as the actual movement of stars, and he failed to appreciate that de la Hire's claim to detection of stellar movement was overwhelmed by the measuring errors.

gravitational attraction of the protostar, these nebular remnants, following Newtonian mechanics, would shrink and flatten out into a nebular disk. In Kant's model, "kernels" would begin to form in the nebular disk. These would collect matter, causing the disk to resolve finally into a number of planets (see Figure 4.1).

By the start of the following century, virtually all astronomers and physicists adopted some form of Kant's primal nebula theory for the evolution of the universe. Consequently, Kant garnered the title "father of modern cosmology."

Kant knew full well that by conceiving the universe to be in continual process of mechanistic evolution, he was relegating the Deity to prime mover, at best. He even tried to include strictly mechanistic biological evolution as an extension of his nebular hypothesis, but he eventually abandoned the attempt for want of a clear understanding of the internal processes of living organisms.[5-7]

Six years after the publication of Kant's theory for the heavens, Jean Lambert resurrected, knowingly or not, the ideas of Lucretius (see chapter 2). He proposed that beyond Kant's universe of Milky Ways may lie countless universes of Milky Ways, and beyond that, countless universes of universes of Milky Ways, and so on, ad infinitum. Lambert's idea, his suggestion of a truly infinite universe, spurred Kant to write his *Critique of Pure Reason*.

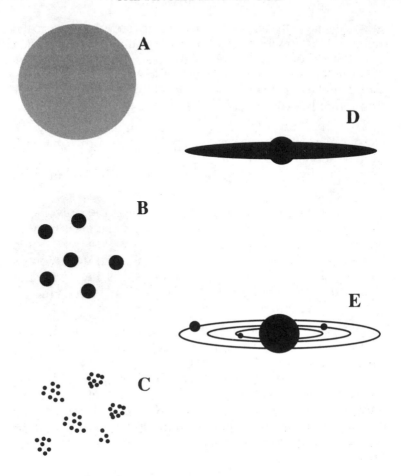

Figure 4.1: Kant's evolution of the universe from a primal nebula

The universe (A) begins as an aggregate of randomly moving molecules. This primal nebula condenses into several smaller nebulae (B). Within each smaller nebula (C) small cores of mass attract other molecules thereby collapsing the nebula into clusters of protostars. Nebular remnants surrounding a protostar (D) contract under gravity and under conservation of angular momentum to form a disk. Kernels within the nebular disk (E) collect matter, eventually transforming the disk into protoplanets.

Kant's theology

In *Critique of Pure Reason* and in his other works, including *Critique of Practical Reason, Critique of Judgment, Only Possible Ground of Proof for the Being of God, Religion Within the Limits of Reason Alone,* and *Dreams of a Spirit Seer,* Kant more fully developed and explained the theological foundation for his cosmology. He began by sweeping away all accepted proofs for the existence of God,[c] both the philosophical proofs of Augustine and Aquinas and the newer rational developments on these proofs by Kepler, Newton, Lessing, and Herder.[8 - 10] And his reasoning seemed utterly plausible to his peers. Though he credited his success to the logic of his arguments, his forceful assertion of assumed "truths" was more likely responsible.

Kant's most directly stated axiom is that knowledge can be obtained only through the human senses of sight, hearing, touch, taste, and smell. That is, only sensory things can be apprehended. A corollary to this axiom, first stated by David Hume, is that a cause can never be proved from its effect. Another corollary is that man has no innate ideas. A third corollary is that no existence beyond the humanly experienced dimensions of length, width, height, and time can be known. By logical deductions from these three corollaries Kant believed he had shattered each of Augustine's and Aquinas' "irrefutable" proofs for God.

Kant rejected the possibility of absolutes, though, ironically, he set forth his axiom and corollaries as absolutes. In his early writings he denied that time and space, in and of themselves, are *real* entities. In one section of his critiques on antinomies on pure reason he stated that "no experience of an absolute limit, and consequently no experience of a condition which is itself absolutely unconditioned, is discoverable."[11] In *Religion Within the Limits of Pure Reason Alone,* Kant explains that

---

c. I am speaking of God in the Judeo-Christian sense as a personal being separate from His creation.

31

any absolute entity leads us into mysteries transcending human concepts, mysteries therefore unsuited to man's comprehension.[12]

It becomes obvious, then, why Kant flatly denied the comprehension of anything supernatural. According to Kant, miracles are illusory since they involve "the possibility of our overstepping the bounds of our reason in the direction of the supernatural (which is not, according to the laws of reason, an object of either theoretical or practical use)."[13]

Thinking that he had thus swept aside the possibility of discovering or knowing any divine agency in the universe, Kant, nevertheless, refused to be known as an atheist. He freely admitted to being awed by the starry heavens above and by the living organisms around him. However, he defined "God" simply as the moral disposition within man which is "the basis and interpreter of all religion." This moral disposition has nothing to do with God-ordained standards of right and wrong, of good and evil, but credits man with doing good for his own benefit—for his own survival. Kant's "theology," hence, is nothing more than moral anthropology.[d]

On careful examination, Kant's arguments for the unknowability of God's existence prove circular. Each of his axioms and its corollaries is derived simply from the underlying assumption that God cannot communicate with man, an assumption that Kant never addressed. Paradoxically, few scholars have even questioned Kant's underlying assumption, despite its implausibility. Would a God wise and powerful enough to create the universe be incapable of communicating with man?

---

d. Kant unequivocally claimed to be a theist. His only basis for proof of God's existence, however, was his highly subjective construction of the moral argument. By denying all objective evidences for God, Kant provided much of the foundation for nineteenth and twentieth century agnosticism.

Immanuel Kant (1724-1804), "father of modern cosmology," supposedly refuted the classical cosmological arguments for the existence of
God and, thus, swayed Western thought towards agnostic and
atheistic world views (photo courtesy of Brundy Library).

Kant's cosmological refinements

In the years following the formulation of his
theological axiom and corollaries, Kant returned to his
work on cosmological models. He had once considered
two possibilities,

either that "the universe has a beginning in time and
is also limited in regard to space,"

or that "the universe has no beginning and no limits
in space, but is—in relation both to time and
space—infinite."[14]

By switching back and forth from the empirical level to
the postulational, Kant made this antinomy appear unre-
solvable. Upon this apparent irresolution he founded his

most celebrated disproof of the cosmological arguments of Augustine and Aquinas. However, in due time, he personally opted for the latter part of the antinomy.

Kant now simply plagiarized[e] Giordano Bruno's argument that experience of either a void time or a void space is impossible. Hence, he proceeded to work from the assumption of infinitude.[15, 16] His models, thus, were governed by his concepts of space, time, and infinity, but more fundamentally by his assumptions concerning the impossibility of discovering any "first event," or creation out of nothing, for the universe.[f]

outline of Kant's cosmology

In summary, Kant began with an unstated fundamental axiom: God's existence is not provable.

Therefore, he deduced,

1. man's knowledge is limited to that which he can obtain through the five human senses,

2. a cause can never be proved from its effect,

3. man has no innate ideas,

4. no existence beyond the humanly experienced dimensions can be proved,

5. no absolute can ever be established to exist, and

6. miracles are illusory and cannot be proven.

---

e. Plagiarism was tolerated much more in the eighteenth century than in the twentieth.

f. Ironically, Kant in 1755 concluded on the basis of God's existence that the universe must be infinite, claiming: "It is evident that in order to think of it [the universe] as in proportion to the power of the Infinite Being, it must have no limits at all ... It would be absurd to represent the Deity as passing into action with an infinitely small part of His potency."[17] Then, in the 1780's, he inferred that if God cannot be proven to exist, the universe must be infinite, as well as the converse, that an infinite universe means that God cannot be proven to exist!

Hence,

a. the development of the universe is strictly mechanistic,

b. the universe has no beginning in time,

c. the universe is infinite in extent,

d. time and space are strictly relative, and

e. everything about and in the universe can be explained by the laws of physics.

Conclusion: The question of God's existence lies beyond the reach of man's knowledge.

Kant's influence on science

Immanuel Kant's theology and cosmology not only dominated astronomical thinking in the latter half of the eighteenth century, but they cast a shadow across the whole of the nineteenth and a large fraction of the twentieth centuries. This influence resulted, in part, from developments in observational astronomy that seemed to support Kant's notions and that demanded a specialist's knowledge of physics and mathematics. Theologians and philosophers increasingly left serious study of cosmology to astronomers and physicists.[g]

These astronomers and physicists, even less aware of Kant's underlying presuppositions than were the theologians and philosophers, rarely questioned Kant's axiom and corollaries. In fact, for the next two hundred years, astronomers and physicists tended to treat cosmology as a purely scientific discipline without theological or philosophical roots and implications. Kant's claim that cosmology can be treated strictly mechanistically went unchallenged, for the most part.

---

g. Consider, for example, Engelbert Schücking's statement, "We have been able to scare most of the ministers out of cosmology by a straightforward application of tensor analysis."[18]

empirical support for Kant's cosmology

What most effectively fueled enthusiasm for Kant's cosmology was the seemingly overwhelming confirmation provided by advances in observational astronomy. Support for the "island universe" hypothesis came early in the 19th century from Britain's foremost astronomer, William Herschel. Herschel set out to map the heavens by counting stars in different directions. In this manner he deduced that the sun is, indeed, part of a giant lens-shaped system of stars.

Observations made through progressively larger telescopes revealed an ever multiplying number of faint stars and faint nebulae. No matter how much farther into space the newer telescopes penetrated, the universe appeared the same—no hint of boundary, no hint of change. When many of the faint nebulae were resolved into stars, infinitude seemed certain. A glimpse at the billions of stars and thousands of nebulae radically stretched the imagination, and powerfully suggested limitless stars spread throughout a limitless space.

theoretical support for Kant's cosmology

Newton's infinite universe model enjoyed unparalleled acclaim. Newtonian laws of motion were shown to apply up to the limits of observational error for every object—planet, star, or nebulae—that the astronomer cared to measure. For example, the motions predicted by Newton's laws for satellites, planets, comets, stars, star clusters, galaxies, or galaxy clusters all hold true, and for all time durations. So precise are these calculations that the measured departures of Uranus from its elliptical orbit about the sun led John Adams and Urbain Leverrier in 1846 to predict successfully and independently not only the existence of another planet (Neptune), but also its position in the sky.[19, 20]

The only serious objection of that era to a universe infinite in extent and age came from the riddle of the dark night sky. This riddle caught the attention of Thomas Digges in 1576,[21] but was first presented as a paradox by Edmund Halley in 1715. Halley calculated that the night sky would be bright, not dark, if the universe contained an infinite number of stars.[h, 22] P. L. de Cheseaux in 1744 and Heinrich Olbers in 1823 were thought to have resolved the paradox by hypothesizing absorption of light by an interstellar medium. When the first photographs of the Milky Way taken late in the nineteenth century revealed dark cloud-like structures next to dense clusters of stars, their hypothesis seemed confirmed. Final proof that star light indeed was dimmed appreciably by these interstellar clouds was given in 1930 by Robert Trumpler.[23]

influence of Kant beyond cosmology

As the accumulating evidence for Kant's infinite universe model lent credence to Kant's theological and philosophical axioms and corollaries, these "truths" began to affect far more than just cosmology. In the decades since the publication of Kant's works, the tenets he delineated have served as the foundation for many of the "isms" that still dominate the thinking of our time (see Table 4.1).

---

h. The apparent brightness of any light source diminishes by four times for every doubling of its distance. Assuming evenly spaced stars, every doubling of distance increases the volume, and hence the number of stars, by eight. But, the received light from each star decreases by only four. Thus, the received starlight doubles with each doubling of distance. Continued indefinitely, Halley reasoned, the accumulated starlight must become infinite.

Table 4.1: Modern "isms" based (at least in part) on Kant's philosophical assumptions
(see section, *outline of Kant's cosmology*, pages 34-35)

behaviorism	liberationism
existentialism	Marxism
fascism	neo-Darwinism
Freudianism	nihilism
hedonism	pragmatism
humanism	relativism

The list in Table 4.1 is by no means complete, but it gives an indication of the breadth of Kant's impact. Obviously, the credibility of Kant's axiom and corollaries is of utmost importance, not just to scientists and theologians, but also to economists, politicians, sociologists, psychologists, educators, and, for that matter, the rest of the human race.

CHAPTER FIVE

Scientists Rediscover God

summary

Toward the end of the nineteenth century, evidence against the infinite universe model was accumulating but receiving little or no attention. Einstein's special relativity laid the foundation for his general relativity, which demonstrated that the universe must be both decelerating and expanding. Deceleration and expansion together imply that the universe is finite, that the universe has an origin, a beginning, which in turn suggests some causal agent, or "Creator."

early evidence against Kant's cosmology

Throughout the nineteenth century the general reliability of Newton's laws of mechanics and Maxwell's equations for electromagnetics was demonstrated so repeatedly and widely that scientists believed them applicable to all natural phenomena. Near the close of the century, physicists were feeling smug. The majority held the opinion that all that was left for their successors was merely to "make measurements to the next decimal place." No significant cosmological developments were anticipated, and the Newtonian infinite universe model was cast in concrete.

However, this tranquil situation prevailed only for a brief season. A lasting disturbance came from three unexpected discoveries in physics and astronomy:

39

1. *heat transfer by radiation*

In 1879 Josef Stefan's experiments showed that for any given body the rate of energy radiated from all wavelengths combined increases proportionately with the temperature of the body to the fourth power (W = σT^4). Five years later Ludwig Boltzmann, working independently, derived the same conclusion from statistical mechanics. In general, radiant energy is both emitted from and absorbed by the surface of a body. The difference between the rates of emission and absorption is simply the rate of heat transfer. It then follows from the laws of thermodynamics that, given enough time, a body will assume the temperature of its surroundings and, therefore, radiate away as much energy as it receives.

This finding implies that Halley's objection to an infinitely large and infinitely old universe still stands. The solution proposed by de Cheseaux and Olbers, the claim that an interstellar medium absorbs the excess light from infinitely distant stars, fails; for the medium in the process of absorption must reach a temperature at which it radiates as much light as it receives. Incredibly, this explanation, though its principles were routinely taught in undergraduate physics courses from the 1890's onward, was not applied to de Cheseaux's and Olbers' work until 1960.[1]

2. *gravitational potential paradox*

Not until 1871 did anyone formally attempt to calculate the gravitational potential within an infinite Newtonian universe. In that year Johann Friedrich Zöllner demonstrated that at any point within an infinite, homogeneous universe the gravitational potential would be infinite—a conclusion at odds with all observations. However, despite Zöllner's fame as professor of astrophysics at Leipzig, his objection to the infinite Newtonian universe received no attention. Only when his objection was independently raised by Hugo Seeliger in 1895 and by Carl Neumann in

1896 did astronomers acknowledge a significant problem.[2] Still, rather than abandon the Newtonian model, Seeliger and Neumann sought to save it by introducing ad hoc[a] an exponential factor to modify Newton's equations in such a way as to generate cosmical repulsion at large distances.

3. *Michelson-Morley Experiment*

Physicists of the 1880's were convinced, on the basis of Maxwell's equations, that "light propagates with a fixed velocity relative to an all-pervading æther."[3] The aberration of starlight (slight cyclical shift in apparent star positions related to the earth's orbital motion), first observed in 1728, proved that this "æther" cannot travel with the earth.[4, 5] On the basis of that discovery, two American physicists, Albert Michelson and Edward Morley, proceeded to determine the absolute velocity of the earth in the æther by measuring the speed of light in different directions and at different positions of the earth in its orbit about the sun. To their astonishment, the experiment (made in 1887) failed to reveal any motion of the earth at all.

For almost twenty years physicists attempted to patch up the classical theories. They proposed wild hypotheses. One suggested that all material bodies contract in the direction of motion. Another that the velocity of a light wave remains associated with the velocity of its source. Various experiments and astronomical observations, however, forced the rejection of all these desperate stabs.

Any one of these three discoveries should have been sufficient in itself to throw the infinite Newtonian universe model onto the trash heap. However, so strong was the emotional attachment of most scientists to Kantian presuppositions and so confident were all scientists in

a. By *ad hoc* I mean "without observational or experimental support," motivated by no other purpose than to save a hypothesis.

Newton's gravitational theory, that the century closed with the infinite Newtonian universe model as dogmatically preached and zealously guarded as ever.

special relativity

As the twentieth century dawned, the only conclusions consistent with all observations of the velocity of light were these two:

1. There is no absolute reference system from which absolute motions in space can be measured.
2. The speed of light with respect to all observers is always the same.

In 1905 Albert Einstein, who at that time worked as an engineer in the Swiss patent office and studied physics in his spare time, conceded these conclusions in his paper on the theory of special relativity.[6, 7] Further, he derived equations which revealed by exactly how much two observers moving with respect to one another would disagree on their measurements of length, velocity, mass, and time. Typically, the equations of classical physics would need to be multiplied by the dilation or expansion factor,

$$\Delta = 1/\sqrt{(1 - v^2/c^2)} \tag{5.1}$$

where v is the velocity of one observer with respect to the second, and c is the speed of light. However, since the velocity of light is so enormous, measurements of length, velocity, mass, and time remain unaffected for "normal" low-velocity physics.[b]

b. Because of the immensity of the speed of light, the dilation factor $1/\sqrt{(1 - v^2/c^2)}$ has been measurable for only the last hundred years. For a high speed locomotive the correction factor is less than a trillionth of a percent. Even when astronaut John Glenn orbited the earth at 18,000 mph, the correction to his elapsed time of travel amounted to less than a ten thousandth of a second.

Applying this dilation factor to the classical expressions for momentum and to Newton's law of force, one can easily derive[8] that matter can be entirely converted into energy, and energy into matter, according to the following equation:

$$E = mc^2 \qquad (5.2)$$

where **m** is the mass at rest and **E** is the energy.

Einstein is to be credited more with audacity than with genius. The theory of special relativity should have followed within months, or at most a year or two, of the Michelson-Morley experiment. However, Newtonian and Maxwellian physics and the cosmology they seemed to support were held in such awe that to suggest an entirely new way for describing phenomena within the universe was considered impudent. In other words, emotional resistance kept Einstein's theory at bay.

experimental proofs

Finally, that resistance to Einstein's theory broke when experiments and observations confirmed all of its dilation predictions. Even before the theory of special relativity emerged, an increase in mass for moving electrons had been observed.

In 1909 the dependence of electron mass on velocity (according to equation 5.1) was verified for electron velocities from 0 to 0.7c, and since then for velocities up to 0.99c and beyond. Further testing showed the lifetimes of unstable particles, such as mesons, to be dilated in perfect agreement with equation 5.1. In 1921, during the first experiments in artificial radioactivity, Ernest Rutherford confirmed the validity of equation 5.2. Much better known are the measurements of mass conversion into energy in nuclear reactors and bombs, also the publicized clock experiments on orbiting space craft.

The success of Einstein's equations in predicting all manner of observations and experiments[9, 10] was overwhelming. In fact, in 1986 one experiment[11] successfully demonstrated the correctness of the relativistic dilation factor (equation 5.1) to within one part in 10^{21}. These confirmations have led to universal acceptance of the validity of special relativity.[c]

general relativity

The triumph of special relativity gave Einstein the boldness in 1915 to extend his theory beyond velocity effects and on to the acceleration effects between observers.[12, 13] Widely advertised as beyond the comprehension of all but a few brilliant scientists, general relativity, nonetheless, has cosmological implications that can be understood by all. To be sure, the foundational equations of general relativity may seem intimidating. But, if one is willing to put aside his/her fears for the moment and plunge ahead, a surprising simplicity awaits.

Given that matter spreads uniformly (at least roughly so) throughout the universe, then the behavior of the universe over time (including its origin and termination) is described by the following equations:[d]

---

c. Most creationists holding to Ussher's chronology for Genesis still reject special relativity. These individuals, in spite of potent and plentiful contrary evidence, insist that *no* adjustments to classical physics are necessary. Their rejection of special relativity seems to arise from their reaction of its implications—extragalactic distances, stellar aging processes, general relativity, and the big bang—all of which require a time scale of billions of years for the creation.

d. No distinction between space and time exists in relativity. Thus, to be universally applicable these equations must be formulated in four-dimensional geometry. Readers familiar with tensor calculus may find this formulation in *Gravitation and Cosmology* by Steven Weinberg (New York: John Wiley, 1972), pp. 151-157. It is explained in "Lectures on General Relativity" by Alfred Schild, in *Relativity Theory and Astrophysics I. Relativity and Cosmology*, ed. by Jürgen Ehlers (Providence, RI: Am. Math. Soc., 1967), pp. 20-73.

$$2(d^2R/dt^2)/R + [(dR/dt)/R]^2 + kc^2/R^2 = -8\pi Gp/c^2 \quad (5.3)$$

$$[(dR/dt)/R]^2 + kc^2/R^2 = 8\pi G\rho/3 \quad (5.4)$$

where **R** is the scale factor for the universe (basically its length or diameter), **t** is time, **k** is a constant describing the geometry of the universe, **c** is the speed of light, **G** is the constant of gravity, **p** is the total pressure arising from all sources, and ρ is the density of matter and radiation. The terms **dR/dt** and **d²R/dt²** simply represent velocity and acceleration in calculus notation.[e]

observable consequences

With his general theory of relativity Einstein predicted three observable effects:[14, 13]

1. gravitational deflection of starlight by the sun,

2. perihelion advance[f] of a body orbiting between the sun and the earth, and

3. gravitational red shift[g] of spectral lines.

All three follow from the theory's requirement that gravity must alter the properties of space and time.

During the May 1919 total solar eclipse, British astronomer and mathematician Arthur Eddington catapulted Einstein to worldwide fame. Eddington and his colleagues determined that starlight was bent by the sun's gravitational field by 1.8 ± 0.2 arcseconds.[h] Einstein's theory had predicted a bend of 1.751 arcseconds.[15]

---

e. These equations do not appear exactly as Einstein wrote them in 1915. Rather, they include a correction made by Alexander Friedmann in 1922. This correction is discussed on page 56.

f. The perihelion is the point in the orbit of a body (such as a planet or an asteroid) where that body is nearest to the sun.

g. The gravitational redshift is the shifting of a spectral line of a body toward a longer wavelength by the gravitational field of that body.

h. One arcsecond is 1/3600th of a degree or about .06 percent of the angular diameter of the moon.

Even before the publication of observational proofs of general relativity, astronomers were aware of an unaccounted for 42.6 ± 0.9 arcseconds per century advance in the perihelion of Mercury's orbit. The 43.03 arcseconds-per-century advance predicted from general relativity provided the most unambiguous mark of the theory's predictive accuracy.

Through the years the general theory of relativity has been confirmed by the observational tests proposed by Einstein, and other effects derived since, to better than one-hundredth of a percent precision. A summary of results from observational tests is given in Table 5.1. Needless to say, so much evidence now has been accumulated that no one seriously doubts the validity of the general theory of relativity.

Table 5.1: Observational verifications of general relativity

The symbol Δ means "change in," and the symbol " means "arcseconds." Hence, ΔP means change in the period, while Δν means change in the frequency (inverse of the wavelength). Note that the periastron advance for the pulsar PSR 1913+16 is more than 35,000 times greater than the perihelion advance for Mercury.

1. comparison of theoretical and observed centennial precessions of planetary orbits[16]

planet	general relativity	observations
Mercury	43.03"	43.11"±0.45
Venus	8.6"	8.4"±4.8
Earth	3.8"	5.0"±1.2
Icarus	10.3"	9.8"±0.8

2. gravitational deflection of starlight[17]

general relativity: 1.751"   observations: 1.70"±0.10

3. gravitational deflection of radio signals from quasars[18]

general relativity: 1.751"   observations: 1.73"±0.05

4. radar measurement of Mercury's perihelion advance[19]

    general relativity: 43.03"   observations: 43.20"±0.30

5. rate of advance of periastron for the binary pulsar[i] PSR 1913+16[20, 21]

    general relativity: $4.2°±0.3$/yr   observations: $4.225°±0.002$/yr

6. orbital period change due to gravitational radiation for the binary pulsar PSR 1913+16[21]

$$\Delta P_{experiment}/\Delta P_{theory} = 1.13±0.19$$

7. echo delays of laser signals reflected from Apollo-placed corner cube reflectors on the moon[22]

    general relativity β parameter = 1.0   observations: 1.003±0.005

    general relativity γ parameter = 1.0   observations: 1.008±0.008

8. gravitational red shift of spectral lines on the earth's surface (Mössbauer effect)[23]

$$\Delta\nu_{experiment}/\Delta\nu_{theory} = 0.9970±0.0076$$

9. gravitational retardation of radio signals[24]

    general relativity γ parameter = 1.0   observations: 1.000±0.001

10. gravitational red shift of the neutral hydrogen spectral line[25]

$$\Delta\nu_{experiment}/\Delta\nu_{theory} = 1.000000±0.000070$$

11. gravitational lens effect on quasar[j] images[26 - 29]

---

i. Pulsars are the collapsed remains of exploded stars (supernovae—see footnote k in chapter 9). In the process of collapsing from a several million mile diameter star down to an object just a few miles across, the rotation period of the star spins up to where it rotates once every few seconds (in some cases once every few milliseconds). Since the axis of spin and the axis for the star's magnetic field typically do not coincide, radiation associated with the magnetic field, to a distant observer, will appear to pulsate on and off as the star rotates.

j. The quasars are the most powerful known bodies in the universe. Some of them emit the energy flow of over a thousand normal galaxies from a volume only one trillionth the size of a normal galaxy. Most of the quasars are located at distances beyond a billion light years.

Albert Einstein (1879-1955) in his theory of relativity demonstrated the falsehood of Kant's philosophical notions about the universe and consequently took an important role in reversing the trend towards agnosticism and atheism (photo courtesy of The Bettmann Archive).

physical implications

An interesting physical consequence results from merely subtracting (or canceling out) equation 5.4 from 5.3. The remainder is

$$2(d^2R/dt^2)/R = -8\pi G(\rho + 3p/c^2)/3 \qquad (5.5)$$

Since the constant of gravity is of positive value, this remaining equation states that the universe is decelerating.

universe is much smaller than the density. For all practical purposes, then, the pressure can be set equal to zero. Straightforward calculus solutions of equation 5.5 yield the result that **R** (the size factor) can progress in three possible ways:

1. increasing indefinitely with time,
2. increasing ever more slowly, or
3. increasing to a maximum value and then decreasing.

In other words, the universe must be expanding, or it has been expanding in the past.

theological implications

While general relativity implies an age for the universe vastly beyond 6,000 years,[k] it also implies that there is, indeed, a creation date. Expansion, coupled with deceleration, indicates a universe that is exploding outward from a point. In fact, through the equations of general relativity, we can trace that "explosion" backward to its origin, an instant when the entire physical universe burst forth from a single point of infinite density. That instant when the universe originated from a point of no size at all is called the *singularity*.[l] No scientific model, no application of the laws of physics, can describe what happens before it. Somehow, from beyond itself the universe came to be. It began. It began a limited time ago. It is finite, not infinite.

---

k. Proponents of Archbishop Ussher's date for the creation must reject both general and special relativity.[30 - 33] Those who knowingly do so, base their rejection on 1) inaccuracies in the measurements of Eddington *et al.* of the deflection of starlight, and 2) oblateness of the sun as a possible explanation for the perihelion advances of the planets. An abundance of new experimental evidence, however, removes any basis for such arguments (see Table 5.1).

l. The singularity is not really a point. It is the whole of three dimensional space compressed to zero size. This infinitely shrunken space actually represents a boundary at which space ceases to exist.

The implications can only be described as monumental. Atheism, Darwinism, and virtually all the "isms" emanating from the eighteenth to twentieth century philosophies are built upon the assumption, the incorrect assumption, that the universe is infinite.[m] The singularity has brought us face to face with the cause—or causer—beyond/behind/before the universe and all that it contains, including life itself. According to the centuries-old cosmological argument for God's existence,[34]

1. everything that begins to exist must have a cause of its existence;

2. the universe began to exist (a scientifically verifiable fact);

therefore, the universe must have a cause of its existence.

What, then, has been the response of the scientific community, and what was the response of Einstein, in particular?

---

m. The necessary finiteness of the universe required by general relativity applies to its origin in the finite past. It may be spatially infinite. If the universe expands indefinitely with time, and if it is homogeneous and isotropic, then it possibly may contain an infinite amount of matter. For other considerations see the section, "limit of the universe," in chapter 9.

PART TWO

Scientific Cosmology

With the development of research techniques and tools, man began to observe the universe in ever greater depth and detail and, thus, to test his cosmological musings. The results of that research have been surprising, even disturbing, to many investigators, for the observations continue to disclose the fingerprint of the God of the Bible.

CHAPTER SIX

The Expanding Universe

summary

Einstein introduced a cosmological "fudge factor" that would get his equations to yield a static model for the universe. However, subsequent observations of the velocities of distant galaxies and conclusions from thermodynamics proved incontrovertible. The universe is, indeed, expanding.

cosmological constant

Einstein's reactions to his own equations may possibly acknowledge the threat of an encounter with God. Before he published his cosmological inferences from the theory of general relativity, he searched for a way to "fix up" the equations, anything to permit a static solution, a universe free of expansion or deceleration.

Einstein postulated a cosmic force of repulsion to cancel off the attractive force of gravity, despite the body of evidence that gravity was predominant in its influence throughout our galaxy and its vicinity.[1 - 3] Einstein had to develop a repulsive force that would have imperceptible consequences for nearby objects but overwhelming effects over extreme distances. The only way this could be expressed consistently was to add a term, Λ, to the right hand side of equation 5.3, $\Lambda/3$ to the right hand side of equation 5.4, and $2\Lambda/3$ to equation 5.5. In each case Λ represents the cosmical constant of repulsive force, or what Einstein termed the *cosmological constant*. By introducing this constant, he could eliminate both deceleration and expansion.[a] Thus, the inevitability of an ultimate beginning for his model of the universe could be avoided.

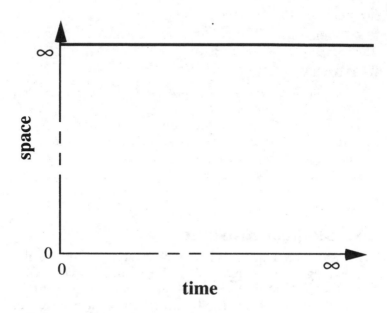

Figure 6.1: Einstein's static universe model

Einstein speculated that a new force of physics (as yet undiscovered) might exactly cancel off the effects of gravity upon the universe. By this hypothetical force, the deceleration and expansion of the universe could be eliminated, and a static, infinitely old and infinitely large universe would be made possible. With such a model the origin of the universe could be placed beyond practical consideration.

theoretical difficulties

The price Einstein was prepared to pay to avoid facing an origin for the universe seems astonishing. His repulsive force constant demanded violations of

---

a. For perfect cancellation of the effects of gravity upon the universe, a value for Λ equal to $4\pi G(\rho + 3p/c^2)$ must be assigned.

established realities. For one, his vacuum would behave similarly to space containing matter, exhibiting gravitational properties and containing energy. For another, his force of repulsion between two bodies would *increase* with increasing separation.

When these properties of the cosmological constant finally were apprehended, most astronomers rejected the term's inclusion in any physical theory.[b] In time, theoreticians found that Einstein's static universe could not be kept static. They demonstrated that the formation of galaxies would cause the static model to become unstable resulting in a quick collapse of the universe.[5 - 8] Further, they observed that the emission of radiant energy in any part of the universe is far in excess of the absorption of energy. This finding means that the universe departs too radically from thermodynamic equilibrium to remain static. Finally, observers demonstrated that the galaxies really are expanding away from one another.

expanding universe

In the same year that Einstein published his static model for the universe (1917), Dutch astronomer Willem de Sitter produced another so-called static solution (the "B solution") for the universe from Einstein's general equations.[9] By setting up the spatial coordinates in a special manner and by adopting a matter content for the universe equal to zero, de Sitter attempted to make his model independent of time. However, the universe is not empty. And, in actuality, de Sitter's solution predicted that the scale of the universe would expand with respect to time. So, in spite of de Sitter's impositions, it was not long before theoreticians and observers alike began to refer to the expansion of the universe as the "de Sitter

---

b. One notable exception was Arthur Eddington who as late as 1930 stated, "On general philosophical grounds there can be little doubt that this form of the equations ($G_{\mu\nu} = \Lambda g_{\mu\nu}$) is correct rather than his earlier form $G_{\mu\nu} = 0$."[4]

effect." By 1928, American mathematician Howard Robertson had inserted the appropriate coordinate transformation, exposing clearly the non-static nature of de Sitter's model.[10]

Unknown to both Einstein and de Sitter, Vesto Slipher disclosed to a meeting of the American Astronomical Society in 1914 his chance discovery that a number of nebulae are receding away from the earth at very high velocities. None of the astronomers present at the meeting appreciated what Slipher's discovery meant. However, one young graduate student, Edwin Hubble, determined not only to identify the nature of the nebulae, but also to solve the mystery of their high recession velocities.

Growing evidence and acknowledgment that distant nebulae may be receding caused a few astronomers to reconsider their philosophical commitments to a static, infinite universe. If the universe were not static, Einstein's awkward cosmological constant would become unnecessary. Moreover, the Russian meteorologist, Alexander Friedmann, in 1922 discovered a simple algebraic error made by Einstein which, once corrected, yielded a clearly non-static solution for the universe.[11]

The Friedmann models are of two types:[11, 12]

1. If the average density of matter in the universe is less than a certain critical value, then the expansion of the universe will go on forever.

2. If the density of the universe exceeds this critical value, then the gravity exerted by the matter eventually will stop the expansion and cause the universe to implode back on itself.

Meanwhile, using the newly-built 100-inch telescope at Mt. Wilson, California, Hubble had by 1923 determined the nature of Slipher's enigmatic receding nebulae. His photographs resolved (for the first time) the Andromeda Nebula into separate stars. In the spiral arms of Andromeda, Hubble measured the periodic variation of some Cepheid variable stars. Since the total radiant power, or luminosity, of a Cepheid variable star is related to its period of variation, Hubble was able to use the observed brightnesses and periods of Cepheid variables to calculate the distance to Andromeda. By this means and other distance-determining methods, he proved that Slipher's receding nebulae lie far beyond our Milky Way galaxy and are, in fact, galaxies in their own right.

Armed with the velocity and distance measurements for many more galaxies (thanks in part to fellow astronomer Milton Humason), Hubble in 1929 announced his famous *law of red shifts*: the more distant a galaxy, the greater, in direct proportion, is its velocity of recession (determined by the shift of its spectral lines to longer, or redder, wavelengths).[13] This observation by Hubble was exactly what the simplest expanding universe model would predict.

Finally, Arthur Eddington and other theoreticians pointed out that the second law of thermodynamics had all along demanded the disintegration of the universe. For the universe as a whole, disorder must continually increase and energy must irreversibly flow from hot to cold bodies. In other words, the universe is running down like a wound up clock. And, if it is running down, then there must have been a time when it was fully wound up.

Thus, classical thermodynamics, observational astronomy, and general relativity joined forces in confirming the maturing of the universe—a maturation with obvious reference to a beginning point and to finite spatial limits. This convergence of research findings was hailed as one of the great triumphs of modern science.[c]

---

c. General relativity predicts that the spatial limits grow as the universe expands. Space began as an infinitely small volume. As the universe expands, space expands with it. Beyond the limits for the universe, space, as we know it, does not exist.

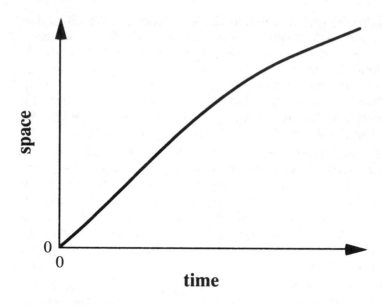

Figure 6.2: Expanding universe model
Einstein's original equations of general relativity imply that all matter, energy, space, and time grows outward from a single point of origin. Later, when it was noted that extreme temperatures would be encountered near the origin, this model began to be called the "big bang."

reaction to theological implications

The concept of an exploding universe seemed to irk the scientific community. Einstein openly fumed over the implications of a beginning point, particularly concerning a Creator or Prime Mover for the universe.[14] Eddington, too, was agitated. He declared the origin of the universe to be "philosophically repugnant."[15, 16] More subtle expressions of irritation came from others such as Omer, who refused to attribute anything special to the time or circumstances of the observer (meaning the observer cannot determine anything about the origin).[17]

Einstein did admit, however, even as early as 1919, that his cosmological constant was "gravely detrimental to the formal beauty of the theory."[18] In 1931, following the publication of Hubble's law of redshifts, Einstein finally discarded the cosmological constant from his field equations and conceded that its introduction was "the greatest mistake of his life."[19]

Einstein gave grudging acceptance to "the necessity for a beginning"[19] and, eventually, to "the presence of a superior reasoning power,"[20] but never did he accept the doctrine of a personal God.[21] Two specific obstacles blocked his way. According to his journal writings, Einstein wrestled with a deeply felt bitterness toward the clergy, toward priests in particular,[22] and with his inability to resolve the paradox of God's omnipotence and man's responsibility for his choices.

> If this being is omnipotent, then every occurrence, including every human action, every human thought, and every human feeling and aspiration is also His work; how is it possible to think of holding men responsible for their deeds and thoughts before such an almighty Being? In giving out punishment and rewards He would to a certain extent be passing judgment on Himself. How can this be combined with the goodness and righteousness ascribed to Him?[23]

Seeing no solution to this paradox, Einstein, like many other powerful intellects through the centuries, ruled out the existence of a personal God.

CHAPTER SEVEN

Cosmic Hesitation

summary

Conflicting data for the age of the universe opened the way for a challenge to the conclusion of a relatively "recent" beginning. Two astrophysicists, one a priest, the other an atheist, suggested this alternative: rather than expanding continuously from an ultra-dense origin, the universe may have hesitated for an indefinite period of time in an intermediate state. Such a model resolved the time scale problem, and in its extreme form gave the possibility of relegating the seeming design characteristics of the universe and life to the work of chance rather than to God.

age dilemma

In the early 1930s an unresolved problem arose to delay acknowledgment that the universe is finite. The age of the universe as calculated from Hubble's measured rate of expansion for the universe was about half the earth's age as determined from radioactive decay.[a] Obviously, a part of the universe could not be older than the whole.

---

a. No concurrent attempts were made by adherents of Ussher's chronology to capitalize on this age problem because it largely was known only by practicing cosmologists.

The method of dating the age of the earth's crust from radioactive decay was well understood even by scientists other than geophysicists.[b] Such measurements were relatively free of systematic errors. Hence, there were no scientific reasons to doubt their validity.

The same could not be said, however, of the Hubble age for the universe. That age estimate came from the slope of the best-fit line through the plot of galaxy distances versus their velocities (see Figure 7.1). This slope represents the speed with which the galaxies are moving away from the earth per unit of distance. For the simplest expanding universe models, the age of the universe is the time it has taken for the galaxies to expand from a single point to their current separation. This age is, therefore, simply the reciprocal of the slope.

Hubble's original measurements for his velocity-distance relation (law of red shifts)[1] are shown in Figure 7.2. The data points definitely indicate some kind of general expansion, but they are too widely scattered to give an accurate measurement. Not only were the distance determinations in most cases imprecise, but they were also subject to several possibly large calibration errors. Hubble did his best to warn the theoreticians against overinterpreting his results.[1, 2] But, most theoreticians failed to appreciate the enormous difficulties (at that time) of measuring extra-galactic distances. So, regrettably, the overinterpretation occurred.

---

b. One can get a feel for this method by noting that radioactive elements decay exponentially such that only one half of the original amount of the element remains after a period of time called the half-life. The fact that radioactive elements of half-lives of billions of years exist on the earth (e.g. thorium and uranium) shows that the earth's age cannot be much greater. On the other hand, the absence of most radioactive isotopes of shorter half-lives (e.g. neptunium) indicates that the earth's age cannot be much less.

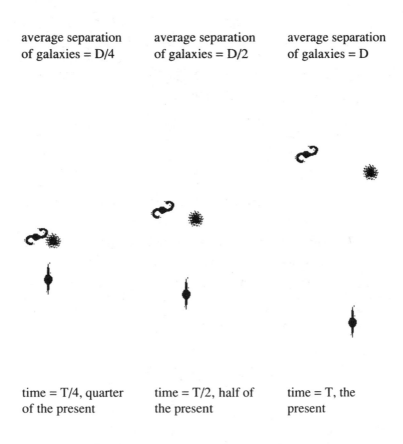

average separation of galaxies = D/4 average separation of galaxies = D/2 average separation of galaxies = D

time = T/4, quarter of the present time = T/2, half of the present time = T, the present

Figure 7.1: **Age measurement for the simplest expanding universe model (negligible deceleration)**

The expansion rate = D/T (i.e. separation distance divided by time). Therefore, the age of the universe = D/E. With measurements of the expansion rate and the current average distance between galaxies one can calculate the age of the universe.

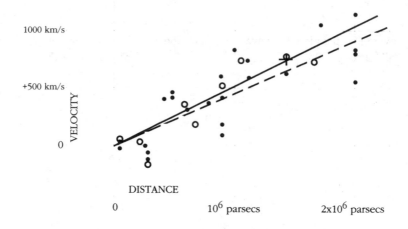

Figure 7.2: Hubble's original velocity-distance relation
(used with permission of the National Academy of Sciences)
The velocities (km/sec.) at which several galaxies are moving away from us are plotted against estimated distances. The cross represents the mean of measurements made on 22 other galaxies. All measurements shown here were made before 1929.

Lemaître's original model

Creatively tackling the age dilemma, Georges Lemaître, a Belgian priest, proposed in 1927 that the general expansion had been interrupted by a near static phase lasting long enough to accommodate the earth's age.[3, 4] In Lemaître's first model (see Figure 7.3) the universe expands rapidly from a singularity,[c] but the density of the universe is such that gravity dramatically slows down the expansion. However, the subsequent

---

c. Many non-static relativistic models have the universe originating from a singularity, a single point of no size at all. However, the singularity is not really a point, but more like a whole three-dimensional space, albeit one of zero size. A zero-sized universe would manifest infinite density and infinitely high temperature.

implosion (predicted by Friedmann) is avoided through a judicious reintroduction of Einstein's cosmological constant and a careful choice of its value. This constant is set so that just when gravity is taking the steam out of the cosmic explosion, the repulsive force is building up to cancel off the effects of gravity. Hence, the expansion is slowed down almost to a standstill, and the universe enters a quasi-static period. But, eventually, the cosmological repulsion begins to dominate. The universe starts expanding again and it continues to expand at an accelerating rate.

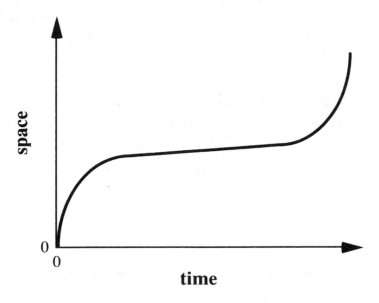

Figure 7.3: Expansion of the universe according to Lemaître's original model

The universe begins by expanding from a singularity. By carefully selecting the values for the density of the universe and the cosmological constant, the expansion of the universe can be slowed down for an arbitrary period of time. In this manner the age of the earth can be accommodated in spite of Hubble's estimate for the expansion rate of the universe.

As Figure 7.3 indicates, the creation date for the universe, assuming uninterrupted expansion according to the rate measured in 1929 and 1931, would be too recent. But, the origin of the earth could easily be placed within Lemaître's quasi-static period. Hence, the age dilemma would be resolved.

Lemaître pointed out an added (supposed) bonus. He claimed that his model was better suited to survive galaxy formation than the static model of Einstein. He argued that since the formation of condensations (protogalaxies) reduces the pressure of the universe, and since the pressure affects gravity, the balance between Λ and gravity proposed by Einstein's model could not be maintained.[5, 6] The imbalance, rather, would give rise to the expansion predicted by Lemaître's model.

Eddington's infinite age refinement

Though he independently verified Lemaître's conclusion concerning the instability of Einstein's model,[7] Arthur Eddington, nonetheless, remained agitated:

> The difficulty of applying this case [Lemaître's expansion] is that it seems to require a sudden and peculiar beginning of things.[8]

> Philosophically, the notion of a beginning of the present order of Nature is repugnant to me. ... I should like to find a genuine loophole.[9]

Eddington worked hard to create a loophole. He stretched Lemaître's quasi-static period to infinity (see Figure 7.4), putting that "repugnant" beginning point all but out of the picture:

> We allow evolution an infinite time to get started; but once seriously started its time-scale of progress is not greatly different from case (b) [Lemaître's expansion].[8]

In pushing the beginning of the universe into the infinite past, Eddington thought he had removed it—and any need for a Creator—from philosophical consideration.

In giving "evolution an infinite time to get started," God might be rendered unnecessary.[d] The improbable self-assembly of the universe and its life-forms conceivably could take place in what appears to be an infinite number of chances afforded by the infinite time scale.

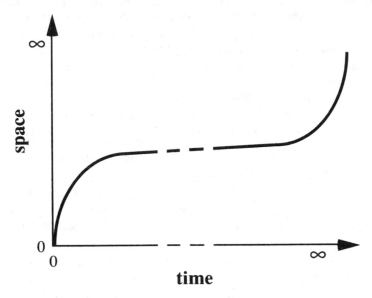

Figure 7.4: Eddington's infinite hesitation model

Eddington discovered that there was one value of the cosmological constant that would permit the stretching of Lemaître's quasi-static period to infinity. He thought, therefore, that philosophically this would remove the notion of a beginning for the universe.

---

d. A flaw in Eddington's argument which should have been discerned by his contemporaries is that even if the origin of the universe is pushed indefinitely into the past, this does *not* yield an infinite amont of time for evolution. Life requires stars and planets, and only a finite number of generations of stars is possible before all the nuclear fuel in any comoving volume of space is eshausted.

the primeval atom

While conceding that Eddington's proposition was theoretically possible, Lemaître could not give it his wholehearted support.[10, 11] He reserved his enthusiasm for yet another alteration. Picking up on Eddington's presumption that the universe might begin with a specific non-zero radius,[8] Lemaître conjectured that the present universe came from the disintegration of a single atom:

> We could conceive the beginning of the universe in the form of a unique atom, the atomic weight of which is the total mass of the universe. This highly unstable atom would divide in smaller and smaller atoms by a kind of super-radioactive process.[11]

> At the origin, all the mass of the universe would exist in the form of a unique atom; the radius of the universe, although not strictly zero, being relatively very small. The whole universe would be produced by the disintegration of this primeval atom.[12]

Up to this time, no satisfactory explanation had been proffered for the origin of cosmic rays or for the source of heavy elements. Through his primeval atom, Lemaître claimed to explain both mysteries.

Lemaître believed that in his primeval atom all the quanta of the universe could be reduced to one quantum wherein space and time would lose any meaning. In other words, he saw his primeval atom model as placing the beginning of the universe before the beginning of space and time. His appeal to Eddington and others was to suggest that "such a beginning of the world [universe] is far enough from the present order of Nature to be not at all repugnant."[10] While steering clear of the blatantly anti-theistic stance of Eddington, Lemaître seemed to be distancing the Creator from the "present order of Nature." However, he may simply have been emphasizing the difference between the "beginning of the world [the universe]" and "the present order of nature."

CHAPTER EIGHT

Steady State Cosmology

summary

Several British astrophysicists suggested that a point of origin for the universe could be avoided by assuming that new matter is continually generated in the spaces between the receding galaxies. The universe, in that case, would appear the same to all observers at all times (even an infinite time) in spite of a general expansion. If the universe were truly infinite in all respects, there would seem to be no need to invoke anything beyond the universe itself to explain its, or our, existence.

The hesitation models of Lemaître and Eddington represent not the only attempts to resolve the age paradox for the universe. During the 1930s and 1940s a number of ingenious theories were proposed to circumvent the difficulty.[1] Of all these alternate hypotheses, however, only one, the steady state theory, ever gained popularity.

The first steady state cosmology had been presented back in 1918 by William MacMillan as he tackled the paradox of de Chéseaux and Olbers. MacMillan suggested that matter is converted into energy in stellar interiors and that radiation, as it travels through empty space, is converted into matter, which later coalesces into stars.[2] If matter and energy were to behave in this manner, the gross features of the universe would appear the same at all times. For whatever reasons, perhaps its lack of dramatic flair, MacMillan's idea gained only passing attention. Continual creation *ex nihilo* stole the show, its introduction prompted by a new astronomical problem.

Jeans' conjecture

In the 1920s the British astrophysicist Sir James Jeans became concerned about a possible age dilemma of much greater magnitude than the one encountered in the measured expansion rate of the universe. Unaware of the tidal effects of differential galactic rotation,[a] he calculated from dynamical considerations that open star clusters in our galaxy require at least a trillion years to break up. Since the breakup of some of these star clusters has been observed to be occurring, our galaxy, and hence the universe, Jeans concluded, must be more than a trillion years old.[3]

Seeking a model to accommodate ages for the star clusters in the trillions of years, Jeans suggested that the universe may have neither a beginning nor an end:

It is difficult, but not impossible, to believe that matter can be continuously in process of creation. ... We are free to think of stars and other astronomical bodies as passing in an endless steady stream from creation to extinction ... with a new generation always ready to step into the place vacated by the old.[4]

As to whence the new matter might arise, Jeans surmised that "the centres of the nebulae [galaxies] are of the nature of 'singular points' at which matter is poured into our universe from some other, and entirely extraneous, spatial dimension."[5]

Jeans proposed a simple observational test of his steady state cosmology. A universe that has no beginning and no end should manifest a "steady" population. That is, the number of stars and galaxies in various stages of development should be proportional to the time required

---

a. In a star cluster those stars nearest to the Galactic center are subject to stronger gravitational forces than stars more distant from the center. Unless the gravitational force of the cluster as a whole dominates, this causes a star at the near edge of the cluster to revolve about the Galactic center at a faster rate than a star at the far edge. The difference in these rates of revolution results in the stars at the far side of a star cluster splitting away from those at the near side.

to pass through these stages. The net result should be balanced numbers of infants and elderly, as well as middle-aged, stars and galaxies.

Perfect Cosmological Principle

For two decades the idea of continual, spontaneous creation received little notice. In 1948, however, it received a large boost as British astrophysicists Hermann Bondi and Thomas Gold committed themselves to affirming what they (and others) called the *Perfect Cosmological Principle*—the notion that the universe presents on the large scale "an unchanging aspect." This principle seemed plausible, at that time, for the most distant galaxies then observed appeared to be substantially the same as the nearest galaxies in both spatial distributions and form. Since they had been forced (by the observational evidence) to concede an expanding universe, and since the Perfect Cosmological Principle required that the density of the universe be held constant, Bondi and Gold were obliged to advocate the perpetual self-creation of matter.[6]

Their universe, although infinitely expanding, would remain "stationary" because the voids are constantly filled by the creation of new matter. This model makes the creation of matter no longer a miracle from the past, but an on-going law of nature that can be tested by observations.

In practice, however, the steady state theory of Bondi and Gold (relative to other steady state theories) yields few quantitative results. The Perfect Cosmological Principle simply says that there is a fixed mean density of matter in the universe and that there is a fixed rate for the generation of matter.

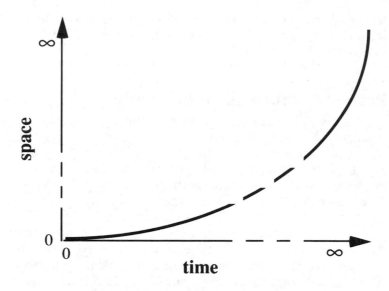

Figure 8.1: The steady state model for the universe

According to the steady state model, the universe, though expanding indefinitely, takes on an unchanging and eternal quality since the voids that result from expansion are filled by the continual spontaneous generation of new matter. Hence, creation of matter need not be a miracle from the finite past, but simply an ongoing law of nature.

Hoyle's C-field

Only three weeks after Bondi and Gold's paper appeared, another British astrophysicist, Sir Fred Hoyle, published a different version of steady state model.[7] Hoyle wanted to formalize creation as a law of physics in such a way that the steady state solution would emerge from Einstein's field equations. Therefore, he invented a creation field, $C_{\mu\nu}$, and simply added it to the left hand side of each of Einstein's original equations for general relativity (5.3 and 5.4).

The physical effect of this addition is that C-field momentum counterbalances the momentum of created particles. In other words, the C-field behaves as a negative (repulsive) energy field and, thus, may provide the driving mechanism for the expansion of the universe. In a steady state universe under the influence of a C-field, the creation rate, the mean density of matter in the universe, the radius of the observable universe,[b] and the expected age of the oldest galaxies within the observable universe all can be derived from the expansion rate for the universe (otherwise known as the Hubble constant).

With the calibration errors in the distance scale for the universe still undiscovered, Hubble's constant was measured in 1948 at 540 kilometers/second/megaparsec (170 kilometers/second/million light years). Using this measurement, Hoyle and yet another British astrophysicist, William McCrea, calculated the following parameters for the C-field steady state model:[8 - 11]

creation rate, $dC/dt = 4 \times 10^{-44}$ gram/centimeter^3/sec.

(about 1 hydrogen atom/liter/billion years)

mean matter density, $\rho = 5 \times 10^{-28}$ gram/centimeter^3

(about 300 hydrogen atoms/meter^3)

radius of observable universe, $R = 2 \times 10^{27}$ centimeters

(about 2 billion light years)

age of oldest observable galaxies, $A_G = 13.4$ billion yrs.

Since the value for this last parameter was close to what then was thought to be the age of the galaxy clusters, Hoyle claimed confirmational evidence for his model.[12]

---

b. The geometry of general relativity is different from Euclidian. The shortest distance between two points becomes a curve rather than a straight line. Therefore, even in the infinite steady state universe model proposed by Fred Hoyle, there remains a spatial limit beyond which observations cannot be made.

THE FINGERPRINT OF GOD

Bondi and Lyttleton's hypothesis

Recognizing a weakness in his and Gold's model in its lack of a mechanism to explain the expansion of the universe, Bondi (working with Raymond Lyttleton) in 1959 suggested that there might be a slight difference in the magnitude of the electric charge of the proton and the electron.[13] If this were the case, there would be a net repulsion between hydrogen atoms, and this conceivably could account for the expansion of the universe. Given a Hubble constant of 100 kilometers/second/megaparsec, a charge difference of only about 1 part in 10^{18} would be required.

nonhomogeneous model

In a series of papers published from 1963-66, Hoyle and Indian theoretician Jayant Narlikar abandoned the assumption of a homogeneous universe.[14 - 18] They discovered that when the **C**-field is applied to a nonhomogeneous (i.e. clumpy) universe, the creation rate becomes large in the vicinity of dense massive objects and small away from them. Since a new **C**-field is generated whenever matter is created, a feedback exists to amplify the process until the repulsive effect of the **C**-field shatters the objects.

The nonhomogeneous steady state model dealt with a few of the observational difficulties threatening the simple model. Since fragmentation and subsequent dispersal of created mass reduces the strength of the **C**-field, one could imagine a region within the universe that expands without creation. If we were living in such a bubble, and if the bubble were large enough, many of the effects of the continual creation process and of the steady state could be hidden from our view. However, if all this were true, it would be impossible to establish that the universe is steady state or that ongoing creation takes place within the observable universe.

What most attracted Hoyle and Narlikar to the nonhomogeneous steady state model, though, was its potential for explaining galaxy formation and very high energy phenomena such as quasars,[c] strong radio sources, and cosmic rays.[d] In their theory, elliptical galaxies would arise from massive inhomogeneities within the expanding bubble. A supercondensed body comprising a billion times the mass of the sun would be able to restrain a total mass of a trillion suns[e] from expanding beyond the dimensions of a typical galaxy.[18] Their theory predicts that high energy particles[f] could be created near highly collapsed massive objects in such a manner as to explain the observed energy output of quasars and the energy spectrum of cosmic rays.[17, 18] However, this model requires an incredibly high coupling constant[g] for the C-field (about 10^{20} times greater than that for the standard steady state model), so high that great difficulties began to arise, even before the end of the 1960s, in reconciling the theory with observable realities.

theological motivations

Hermann Bondi spoke openly of the steady state theory as an expedient tool for answering questions about God, specifically for answering questions about origins. In his book, *Cosmology*, he says that with his steady state

---

c. Quasars are the most powerful known bodies in the universe. Some emit the energy flow of over a thousand normal galaxies from a volume only a trillionth the size of a normal galaxy.

d. Cosmic rays are atomic nuclei (mostly hydrogen) that travel throughout interstellar space at exceedingly high velocities. Their energy spectrum follows a standard power law.

e. A typical galaxy contains about one hundred billion stars, though some contain only a million while others have more than a trillion.

f. By high energy particles astronomers typically are referring to protons and electrons travelling at close to the speed of light.

g. The fundamental forces of physics are governed by coupling constants that express the forces between particles. Therefore, the coupling constant of creation would determine how strongly particles interact with one another through the creation force.

theory "the problem of the origin of the universe, that is, the problem of creation, is brought within the scope of physical inquiry and is examined in detail instead of, as in other theories, being handed over to metaphysics."[19]

Sir Fred Hoyle has never made any pretense about the personal philosophical motivation behind his cosmological models. In the introduction to his 1948 paper, he makes this statement:

> This possibility [steady state] seemed attractive, especially when taken in conjunction with aesthetic objections to the creation of the universe in the remote past. For it seems against the spirit of scientific enquiry to regard observable effects as arising from 'causes unknown to science,' and this in principle is what creation-in-the-past implies.[20]

Hoyle rejected the idea that God must be invoked to explain the existence of the universe. In his book *The Nature of the Universe,* written in 1952, though he admits that "there is a good deal of cosmology in the Bible" and that "it is a remarkable conception," he writes off all religion as a "desperate attempt to find an escape from the truly dreadful situation in which we find ourselves"[21] and Christianity, in particular, as "an eternity of frustration."[22]

Through the years, Hoyle has increasingly broached theological subjects in his writings. In his undergraduate text on general astronomy written in 1975, Hoyle attacks Friedmann's relativistic model on what seem to be wholly theological grounds:

> Many people are happy to accept this position [Friedmann's] ... without looking for any physical explanation of the abrupt beginning of the particles. The abrupt beginning is deliberately regarded as *meta-physical*—i.e., outside physics. The physical laws are therefore considered to break down at $\tau = 0$, *and to do so inherently.* To many people this thought process seems highly satisfactory because a "something" outside of physics can then be introduced at $\tau = 0$. By a semantic maneuver, the word "something" is then replaced by "god," except that the first letter becomes a capital, God, in

order to warn us that we must not carry the enquiry any further. ... I do not believe that an appeal to metaphysics is needed to solve *any problem of which we can conceive*[23] (emphases in the original).

In 1982 he declares his rejection of God by defining the universe as "everything there is,"[24] and the first letter of the word universe becomes a capital, Universe. There is no need, then, to look beyond the universe itself for anything. By so deifying the universe, Hoyle must, of course, argue against its finite age:

> The attribution of a definite age to the Universe, whatever it might be, is to exalt the concept of time above the Universe, and since the Universe is everything this is crackpot in itself. I would argue the need for the Universe to take precedence over time as a knockout argument in favor of a negative answer to the above question. [That question: Did the whole Universe come into being, all in a moment, about ten billion years ago?] ... One could then dismiss cosmologies of finite age because they were offensive to basic logical consistency.[25]

In further support of his semantical proof for "God is identically equal to the universe"[26] (i.e. God is the universe, and the universe is God), Hoyle points out that oppression, suffering, and death are expected, even guaranteed, if strictly natural biological evolution operates, but not if an all-loving, all-powerful God is in charge.[27] There must not be, then, an independent, transcendent being. Like Einstein, he rejects Almighty God for want of a solution to the paradox of sin and suffering.

Hoyle's vigorous argument for a timeless, steady state universe becomes linked, thus, with his "need" to salvage neo-Darwinian evolution.[h] By Hoyle's own admission

---

h. Neo-Darwinian evolution is the belief that advanced life forms developed naturally, as opposed to supernaturally, from primitive forms by hereditary transmission of slight variations and favorable mutations to successive generations. Further, the primitive life forms are held to develop out of the chance assembly of atoms. That is, atoms supposedly evolve into men solely through the agency of the physical laws.

neo-Darwinian evolution would be impossible within a time scale of only ten or twenty billion years:

> I estimated (on a very conservative basis) the chance of a random shuffling of amino acids producing a workable set of enzymes to be less than $10^{-40,000}$. Since the minuteness of this probability wipes out any thought of life having originated on the Earth, many whose thoughts are irreversibly programmed to believe in a terrestrial origin of life argue that the enzyme estimate is wrong. It is—in the sense of being too conservative.[28, i]

Since the evolution of life is fundamental to Hoyle's "faith," he concludes that the only way to deal with probabilities as small as $10^{-40,000}$ is to banish the beginning of the universe and make it everlasting.[33] In the same spirit, Brazilian physicists M. Novello and H. Heintzmann as recently as 1984 justified a revival of the Newtonian analogues to relativistic models (developed by Edward Milne, William McCrea, Otto Heckmann, and Engelbert Schücking[34 - 36]) on no other basis than that $10^{40,000}$ years—or more—would be the minimum time required for the evolutionary development of life.[37]

Obviously, theological presuppositions have played a major role in the design of the steady state models for the universe. Though Hoyle may claim a belief in God, his theism is a semantic maneuver, for he holds to no god beyond the universe itself. The desire to rescue neo-Darwinian evolution from inadequate time scales has clearly been a central factor.

---

i. The improbability of random assembly of life molecules was demonstrated in detail in 1981 by Hoyle and Indian authority on interstellar matter, Chandra Wickramasinghe, in their book *Evolution From Space*.[29] Their conclusion has since been corroborated in even greater detail in *The Mystery of Life's Origin* (1984), in a follow-up paper (1988) by American chemists, Walter Bradley, Randall Kok, and John Taylor,[30, 31] and in *Origins* by yet another American chemist, Robert Shapiro.[32]

CHAPTER NINE

Overthrow of Hesitation and Steady State

summary

Since the 1960s, more than a dozen proofs have matured to verify the expansion of the universe according to some kind of hot big bang model and to negate the hesitation and steady state theories.

resolution of the age dilemma

By the middle 1950s the conflict between the age of the earth and the Hubble age for the universe had been resolved. Through an improved understanding of the relationship between the periods and luminosities of Cepheid variable stars,[a] Hubble's constant of proportionality was drastically revised.[1] Further refinement followed the 1956 publication of an extensive catalog of galaxy

---

a. There are classes of very bright stars for which the period of brightness variation is directly proportional to the intrinsic brightness or luminosity of the star. Therefore, a measurement of the period of light variation for the star yields its true brightness. Comparing this true brightness with the brightness the observer actually sees, gives the distance of the star from the observer. What German-American astronomer Walter Baade discovered was that there were at least three classes of Cepheids each with a different relationship between the luminosity and the period of brightness variation. This distinction, a recalculation of the statistical methods used for determining distances to Cepheids in our galaxy, and the recognition that the dimming of light by interstellar dust had been underestimated resulted in the spectacular announcement that the Hubble age for the universe had been suddenly tripled!

velocities and brightnesses (including updates from the newly completed 200-inch telescope on Mt. Palomar) authored by Mount Wilson astronomers Milton Humason, Nicholas Mayall, and Allan Sandage.[2] With these changes the Hubble constant yielded an age of six to eight billion years for the universe, an age sufficiently older than that of the earth's as to remove the problem.

The recalibration process,[b] however, rolled onward. Allan Sandage, Hubble's student, inherited the project of measuring the rate of expansion for the universe to ever increasing accuracy and to ever greater distances. Gathering data with painstaking care over a period of some thirty years, Sandage and his co-workers determined that Hubble's constant of proportionality was less than half the value adopted in the 1950s.[3 - 6]

A few investigators, notably Gerard de Vaucouleurs and Sidney van den Bergh, for some time have held to a somewhat larger value for Hubble's constant.[7, 8] Recently, however, as the calibration effects have been comprehended more fully, a growing consensus has developed that Hubble's constant lies between 42 and 72 kilometers/second/megaparsec (13 and 22 kilometers/second/million light years).[9 - 14] The most favored value seems to be 55 km./sec./mpc. (17 km./sec./mly.), a value that has remained stable in the research papers of Allan Sandage and Gustav Tammann since 1974.[4, 5, 11, 15]

The Hubble time (the inverse of the Hubble constant), based on the most favored value for the Hubble constant, would be 18 billion years. The Hubble time, however, measures the age of the universe (actually the total amount of time during which the universe has expanded) only if the deceleration in the expansion of the universe is

---

b. Other important factors in the recalibration were these: 1) the apparent magnitude scales used in 1935 were found to be in error, 2) the actual brightnesses of the most luminous stars in large galaxies were discovered to be about four magnitudes brighter than what Hubble assumed, and 3) what Hubble often thought were the "brightest stars" turned out to be HII regions (hot gaseous nebulae several magnitudes brighter than the brightest stars).

negligible. Evidence now is accumulating that the deceleration in the expansion of the universe is more than negligible. With q_0, the deceleration parameter, between +0.1 and +0.2 (currently the favored values[16 - 19]),[c] the age of the universe would lie between 14 and 15 billion years.

limit of the universe

According to the steady state theory, the universe itself would have no actual limit. Its extent would be infinite. The curvature of light due to the influence of general relativity, though, creates a finite spatial limit beyond which earth-based observations cannot be made. Nevertheless, according to general relativity, the red shifts[d] of galaxies and quasars at this finite limit would equal infinity. That is, in a steady state universe, given adequate instruments, galaxy and quasar red shifts all the way out to z = ∞ should be detected.

With the hesitation theory a different kind of red shift limit exists. As Iranian theoretician Vahé Petrosian demonstrated in 1974, very few quasars and galaxies would be expected with red shifts greater than what would be associated with the time back to the quasi-static period.[20] Specifically, red shifts larger than about z = 2.5 would be rare or nonexistent.

Friedmann's expanding universe models could have red shift limits anywhere between 0 and ∞. In all practicality, however, a certain minimum time (after the singularity where z = ∞) is required to form the first galaxies. What is known about galaxy formation time would indicate a red shift limit somewhere between 2 and 20.

---

c. As a function of the scale factor for the universe, **R**, and Hubble's constant, H_0, the deceleration parameter $q_0 = (d^2\mathbf{R}/dt^2)/\mathbf{R}H_0^2$.

d. The red shift, z, of a galaxy or quasar = $\Delta\lambda/\lambda_0$ where $\Delta\lambda$ is the change of spectral line wavelength due to the expansion of the universe and λ_0 is the spectral line wavelength one would measure in the laboratory.

Hence, if it could be demonstrated that galaxies and quasars have a finite red shift limit greater than 2.5 that is independent of observational difficulties, then both the steady state and cosmic pause models would be eliminated. Fortunately, new instruments developed during the 1970s are capable of making such determinations.

On the basis of Petrosian's work and new observations, the hesitation model definitely has been ruled out. Many quasars with red shifts greater than 3.0 have been discovered. The most distant optically selected quasars yet discovered are Q2203+29, Q0051-279, and 1158+4635 with red shifts of z = 4.406, z = 4.43, and z = 4.73 respectively.[21 - 23] The most distant radio selected quasars discovered to date are PKS 1351-018 and PKS 2000-330 with red shifts of z = 3.71 and z = 3.78, respectively.[24, 25]

The steady state models also are contradicted by these findings, specifically by the extreme scarcity of objects beyond red shift 4.[26, 27] Some astronomers believe that a few more objects with red shifts in the range 4.1 to 4.9 will be discovered since the quasar luminosity function appears to differ for one class of quasars.[24, 28, 29] For that one class, namely those with flat power spectra (i.e. where the emitted power at short wavelengths is the same as at long), the number of quasars expected at red shift z = 4 compared to z = 2 is about one-fifth.[24] For most quasars, however, the luminosities drop so sharply with increasing red shift that no red shifts greater than 4 can be found. In any case, the measurable red shift limit for most classes of quasars and galaxies, and a limit that cannot be much beyond z = 4 for the remainder, directly contradicts the predictions of the steady state model.

constancy and linearity of the red shift law

Despite the obsession of many scientists—and even some theologians—to avoid the dramatic conclusion of an expanding universe, no substitute explanation has ever been put forward to account for the red shifts of distant galaxies.[e] All tentatively proposed alternatives have been easily struck down.

The "tired light" hypothesis was one such idea. Several theoreticians suggested that light simply lost energy on its long journey through intergalactic space. However, any energy loss caused by interaction with intergalactic matter would be accompanied by a transfer of momentum and would yield these four effects:[40]

- a smearing of images that increases with distance,

- a broadening of spectral lines that increases with distance,

- a red shifting of radio light a million times further than that of visible light, and

- a dimming of radio light a million times more than that of visible light.

Observations clearly show that none of these effects occurs anywhere within the universe.

There is now no question that the universe expands. Spectral lines of galaxies of all types and at all distances show a consistent wavelength shift toward the red according to the law of redshifts (see discussion in chapter 6). The redshift $\Delta\lambda/\lambda_o$ (where λ_o would be the wavelength if the velocity were zero and $\Delta\lambda$ is the shift in that wavelength due to the actual velocity) is constant in

---

e. While atheistic astrophysicists wanted to avoid the expanding universe model in order to circumvent the creation event, some creationists attacked it in an effort to defend Ussher's chronology for the Bible against the creation time scale required by it.[30 - 32] Harold Slusher, for example, tried to refute the expanding universe by noting that some galaxies exhibit blue shifts.[33] Such galaxies, though, are so close to our own that their random velocities overwhelm the effect of the law of the red shifts. A few creationists even went so far as to "prove" that the velocity of light has decayed.[34 - 37] Not only is their proof scientifically ludicrous,[38, 39] but the 21-cm hydrogen spectral line shows no variation in the velocity of light among galaxies as far away as 14 million light years. Since light from these galaxies took up to 14 million years to reach us, the velocity of light, therefore, has not changed during the last 14 million years.

any given spectrum over 19 octaves of wavelengths.[41] This law of red shifts follows a linear pattern. In fact, in the equation $c\Delta\lambda/\lambda_o = H_o r^n$, where H_o is the Hubble constant, n does not depart from unity by any more than 3 percent over the entire range of observations.[42, 43] In other words, the linearity is firmly established.

This strict linearity of the law of the redshifts implies that every observer regardless of his location within the universe sees the same form of the expansion. This is exactly what one would expect if the universe originated from the infinitely dense singularity inherent in the Friedmann models.

3° Kelvin background radiation

The first to recognize the necessity of the initial conditions of high density and temperature for an expanding universe were William Harkins (1917) and Richard Tolman (1922).[44, 45] In the 1930s, physicists proved that no single density and temperature for the universe could possibly account for the observed distribution and relative abundances of the elements.[46] Based on these (and other) findings, Russian-American physicist George Gamow formally proposed in 1946 his "hot" model of the universe.[47] From the infinitely high temperature of the singularity, Gamow reasoned, the universe would rapidly cool to the point at which protons and neutrons would combine to produce heavier elements. Continued expansion (and cooling) of the universe would arrest this process shortly after the time of origin.

Based on this hot model, Gamow's students, Ralph Alpher and Robert Herman, calculated the ratio of photons to nuclear particles necessary to account for the observed abundances of light elements. From estimates of the cosmic density of nuclear particles, they predicted that the cooling of the "big bang" would yield a faint background radiation with a current temperature of about 5° Kelvin.[48] Their work was published in 1948.

For nearly two decades theoreticians mistakenly surrendered hope of detecting any background radiation temperature so low—only a few degrees above absolute zero. A surprise came in 1965 when scientists at Bell Laboratories—Arno Penzias and Robert Wilson—intending to measure radio emission from our galaxy, calibrated their antenna at 7 centimeters wavelength (where galactic emission is negligible) and found an unexpected excess of about 3° Kelvin in their antenna temperature. This excess did not vary with time of day, year, or direction. The indication was that the entire cosmos must be the source of the mysterious radiation. Amazingly, two cosmologists, Robert Dicke[f] and James Peebles, had just determined that the radiation left over from the big bang would be observable at radio wavelengths of a few centimeters. What they predicted closely matched the excess temperature found by Penzias and Wilson.[49, 50] Since then, this match has been confirmed to much greater precision over a full range of wavelengths.[51, 52]

In other words, the background radiation exactly fits the power spectrum[g] expected for the light and heat produced by a primordial cosmic explosion. Steady state theory proponents have tried desperately to find another explanation, but to no avail.

The specific entropy of the universe provides a second compelling basis for concluding that the background radiation is the remnant of a hot big bang. Entropy measures the degree to which energy in a closed system dissipates, or radiates (as heat), and thus ceases to be available to perform work. *Specific* entropy is the amount

---

f. Dicke had forgotten that back in the 1940's he, himself, had determined that the radiation temperature of the big bang would be a few degrees Kelvin. Having forgotten both his own calculation and that of Alpher and Herman, he was obliged to make a recalculation some two decades later.

g. The primordial cosmic explosion would radiate perfectly, that is, demonstrate complete thermodynamic equilibrium. Therefore, the characteristic power-wavelength pattern of a black body radiator (an idealized, perfectly efficient heat source) would be manifested.

of entropy per individual proton, an amount which for highly entropic systems approximately equals the ratio of photons[h] to baryons.[i] As Table 9.1 shows, the specific entropy of the universe is enormous beyond all comparison. No possible set of astrophysical sources can account for such a huge specific entropy. The hot big bang offers the only reasonable explanation.

Table 9.1: Photon to baryon ratios for several energy sources

A supernova[j] ranks among the most entropic of events possible within the universe. Yet, the entropy of such an event seems meager in comparison to that of the universe, itself.

source	photons ÷ baryons
candle flame	2
fluorescent light tube	1000
the sun (during ten billion years)	1,000,000
a supernova	10,000,000
the universe	1,000,000,000

A third basis for concluding that the cosmic background radiation comes from the big bang is found in its exceptional temperature uniformity. This temperature varies by no more than one part in ten thousand[k] from one direction in the heavens to another.[52, 53] Such ex-

---

h. A photon is the smallest unit of light energy capable of existing independently.

i. A baryon is any of the heavier atomic particles including protons and neutrons.

j. A supernova is a cataclysmic explosion of a massive star in which most of the star is blown off into interstellar space. At the peak of the explosion a supernova can shine forth with almost as much light as an entire galaxy.

k. The only exception to this is a dipolar effect of about one part in a thousand that actually results from a Doppler shift caused by our net motion (towards the Virgo supercluster of galaxies) through the background radiation.

treme uniformity can only be explained if the background radiation comes from remote recesses of space and time.[1]

Given such potent evidence from three different lines of research, most cosmologists consider that the background radiation alone is sufficient proof that the universe began with some kind of hot big bang explosion.

helium abundance

Another confirmation of the big bang came through the measurement of the ambient helium abundance for the universe. In the early 1960s, astronomical observations revealed that the helium content of our galaxy and of other galaxies was not only large (about 27 or 28 percent by mass), but also virtually constant from place to place.[54] If this helium were produced by stars or by other current astrophysical sources, the helium content would vary considerably with location. In 1966, Peebles calculated that the observed abundance of helium precisely matches what would result from nuclear fusion taking place during the first four minutes of the big bang, given the radiation temperature measured by Penzias, Wilson, and others.[55, 56] Peebles' conclusion was confirmed independently by more elaborate calculations done by Robert Wagoner, William Fowler, and Fred Hoyle.[57]

other light element abundances

In addition to accounting for the large amount of ordinary helium, ^{4}He, the hot big bang model also predicts that trace amounts of light elements, namely deuterium (hydrogen with one extra neutron), D, light

---

1. Recent data (1990) from the COBE satellite reveal a uniformity in background radiation that is orders of magnitude higher than any previously measured—further proof that the universe began with some kind of hot big bang. However, the standard big bang model has been ruled out. Instead, the data show a perfect fit with the cold dark matter inflationary big bang.[58 - 60]

helium, ^{3}He, and the lithium isotope ^{7}Li, will be produced in the first few minutes of the expansion of the universe. A recent comparison of big bang nucleosynthesis theory with observations showed a precise match between the predicted and observed abundances of D, ^{3}He, and ^{7}Li.[61]

The steady state theories and cold big bang models (including Lemaître's primeval atom) provide no explanation for the observed amounts of ^{4}He and D. Neither can such models explain the uniform abundances of ^{4}He, D, ^{3}He, and ^{7}Li found throughout the universe.

limits on the cosmological constant

All hesitation models require something other than a zero value for the cosmological constant, Λ. And yet research has continued to counter that possibility. Petrosian's study of the dynamics of galaxy clusters implies that Λ is less than 6 x 10^{-55} per square centimeter.[62]   On the basis of the near linearity of Hubble's law of redshifts, Sandage and Tammann calculated that Λ must be less than about 3 x 10^{-56} per square centimeter.[63]   For the specific case of the cosmic pause models, Petrosian determined that Λ could not exceed 1.3 x 10^{-56} per square centimeter.[64]

In each case we are looking at an extremely small quantity.   In fact, relative to the gravitational constant (units in which c = 1), Λ is less than 10^{-122}. As the British theoretician Stephen Hawking points out, the cosmological constant more accurately measures to be zero than all other physical quantities.[65]   By way of comparison, one of its closest competitors, the mass of the photon relative to the mass of the electron has been measured only to be less than 10^{-24}.   Today, no physicist dares to propose a theory dependent on a non-zero value for the mass of the photon.   By the same token, one must think twice about assigning a value of anything other than zero to a physical ratio measured to be less than 10^{-122}. Hesitation models, therefore, suffer a serious defect.

age of the universe—radioactive isotopes

The very existence of natural radioactive isotopes is evidence that atomic elements are younger than infinity. All natural radioactive elements are daughter products from either Thorium^{232}, Uranium^{238}, Uranium^{235}, or Neptunium^{237}. The radioactive half-lives[m] for these four parent isotopes are given in Table 9.2.

Table 9.2: Radioactive half-lives for the parent isotopes

parent isotope	radioactive series	half-life (years)
Thorium^{232}	4n	1.39×10^{10}
Neptunium^{237}	4n + 1	2.25×10^{6}
Uranium^{238}	4n + 2	4.51×10^{9}
Uranium^{235}	4n + 3	7.07×10^{8}

In 1957, a team of British and American astrophysicists, Margaret and Geoffrey Burbidge, William Fowler, and Fred Hoyle, determined that isotopes of high atomic weight are produced by rapid neutron capture, and that such capture can only occur during supernovae[n] events.[66] Their work and subsequent refinement[67] of it tell us the relative abundances of Th^{232}, U^{238}, and U^{235} at the time of the first supernovae. Comparison of these abundances with current quantities yields the time interval back to when these radioactive elements first were made inside supernovae. Neptunium also would be produced, but none of this element is observed to occur naturally. Therefore, it must have completely decayed away, meaning that the interval back to its genesis exceeds 100 million years.

---

m. Radioactive elements decay exponentially such that only one half of the original amount of the element remains after a period of time called the half-life.

n. The supernova event is the only natural means by which elements heavier than iron can be synthesized.

Measurements of the Th^{232}/U^{238} and U^{235}/U^{238} ratios analyzed by European physicists, F.-K. Thielemann, J. Metzinger, and H. V. Klapdor published in 1983 showed a time span of at least 16.8 billion years, but no more than 22.8 billion years, since the first supernovae.[68] However, William Fowler in a review published in 1987 demonstrated that Thielemann *et al* so overestimated the importance of beta-delayed fission in their calculations that their time spans would need to be reduced by at least 3 billion, and maybe as much as 9 billion years.[69] Subsequently, Thielemann and two colleagues, John Cowan and J. W. Truran, recalculated the time back to the first supernovae as ranging from 12.4 to 14.7 billion years, admitting that calibration errors could add as much as 4 billion years to their estimates.[70] Still more recently, American physicist Donald Clayton examined eight different nucleochronological methods and concluded that supernovae were first formed between 12 and 20 billion years ago.[71]

The time span back to the first supernovae, therefore must be less than 20 billion years. Since the steady state model implies an infinite duration for the universe, it is clearly eliminated. Hesitation models postulating anything other than a short cosmic pause likewise are negated.

age of the universe—the stars

Beginning in the 1950s, astronomers developed the means to determine the ages of stars by matching their observed colors and luminosities with colors and luminosities derived from nuclear burning rates and the conditions that the interiors of stars are in hydrostatic and thermal equilibria. The success with which the theoretical calculations (based on simple physical principles) predicted the observed characteristics of every kind of star and star cluster ranks this work as one of the most extraordinary achievements of modern science. With the advent of high speed computers it has become possible to predict in remarkable detail the observable growth patterns of stars over the broadest range of time periods—from billions, to millions, to thousands, to tens of years, and even to months, days, minutes, seconds, and milliseconds. Understanding of the physics of all manner of star and star cluster variation now is possible.

A complete account of this achievement may be found in a set of textbooks written by John Cox in collaboration with Thomas Giuli.[72] Allan Sandage and Gustav Tammann have written a summary and an update.[5]

The most recent calculations reveal that stars typically shine for billions of years while some are capable of shining for as long as 80 billion years. Therefore, if our galaxy is significantly younger than 80 billion years, a search for its oldest stars should provide an upper limit to its age.

Globular cluster[o] stars turn out to be the oldest entities within our galaxy. The age of the oldest such clusters was calculated by Sandage and by Don VandenBerg to be 17 ± 2 billion years.[73, 74] In a new development, two Canadian teams, one led by James Hesser and another by Robert McClure, have demonstrated that the ratio of oxygen to iron they measured in the clusters 47 Tucanae and M68 would require the subtraction of 3 billion years from the previous age calculations.[75, 76] However, Catherine Pilachowski and Roger Bell have disputed this claim at least for the cluster M92.[77, 78]

While this 3 billion-year disparity still needs resolution, the good news is that color-luminosity fitting in globular clusters now yields age measurements internally precise to ± 0.5 billion years.[75] This method soon should give us an accurate age for our galaxy.

---

o. Globular clusters are spherically symmetric systems of stars typically containing over 100,000 stars each. Their orbits take them far out into the halo of our galaxy. Our galaxy possesses about 120 globular clusters, but some galaxies such as M87 contain over 200.

But, what is the spread of ages for all the galaxies in the universe? American astronomer Donald Hamilton determined that out to a distance of 8 billion light years all galaxies are the same age to within ± 2 billion years.[19] The oldest stars within our galaxy, then, are representative of the oldest stars in the universe. Steady state and long hesitation models fail again.

age consistency

What has thoroughly convinced astronomers that the universe began with some kind of hot big bang and that the steady state and hesitation models are wrong is that three independent lines of research yield a definite and consistent age for the universe. Here is how the age-determining methods work:

1) The universe is older than the age of globular cluster stars by the years needed to form galaxies. Since galaxies and quasars exhibit a red shift limit of $z = 4$ or 5, this means that they do not form until the universe reaches an age where red shifts of 4 or 5 occur. According to a range of reasonable big bang models, this gestation period would lie between 1.4 and 2.0 billion years.[79-81] Thus, the universe is 15 or 18 billion years old.

2) Most theoreticians agree that the collapse of a protogalaxy generates the first supernovae events. The time from the big bang to the start of these supernovae events has been calculated to be, at most, one billion years.[69, 74] Hence, the nucleochronological age of the universe is roughly 17 billion years.

3) As discussed previously, the Hubble age estimate from the law of red shifts, corrected for the deceleration of the general expansion of the universe, is slightly greater than 14 billion years.

A summary of these results, with accompanying error bars, is given in Table 9.3. The exceptional consistency among all the measuring methods is powerful evidence for the finite age of the universe.

Table 9.3: The age of the universe from direct observations

measuring method	age (billions of years)
globular cluster fitting	17.0 ± 2.4
nucleochronology (supernovae)	17.0 ± 4.0
Hubble time	14.5 ± 5.0

mean age = 16.3 ± 3 billion years

middle-aged galaxies

In tackling the steady state and hesitation models astronomers for a long time ignored an amazingly simple argument. It is this: galaxies are *all* middle-aged. There are no newly formed galaxies. Neither are there any extinct varieties. Galaxy formation must have taken place at only one time in the history of our universe. Therefore, the universe cannot be steady state, and, to negate Eddington's proposal, evolution has not had "an infinite amount of time to get started."

This age of the galaxies is confirmed by looking back in time. Since the light from distant portions of the universe took billions of years to reach us, we can view the universe as it was billions of years ago. Such an exercise reveals that the galaxies look progressively younger as one looks farther and farther out into space.

The first observations to verify the more youthful character of distant galaxies were radio source counts done in the 1960s. These studies found that the ratio of the number of radio sources emitting 2 flux units of power compared to the number emitting 9 flux units[p] was six times higher than what was predicted by the steady state models.[82] Since then, the correlation between the age of astronomical objects and their distance has been demonstrated abundantly.[19, 24, 28, 83, 84]

instability of the hesitation models

Research in the 1960s and 1970s also showed that for the hesitation model, instabilities develop during the quasi-static period that force a collapse back into the singularity. If galaxy formation takes place during the quasi-static period, and if this period is very long (say in excess of about 10^{11} years), then the universe suddenly collapses.[70] Thus, either nothing significant happens during the quasi-static period or that period is shorter than about 10^{11} years. Evolution, then, is seriously limited in what it could accomplish during the cosmic pause.

On the other hand, if the quasi-static period exceeds 10^{12} years, then galaxy formation during that period is guaranteed, *but* so is a subsequent collapse back to the initial singularity.[85] Hence, Eddington's infinitely long hesitation is ruled out.

summary of evidence against hesitation and steady state

The evidence marshalled against the long hesitation and steady state models is overwhelming and decisive. Neither model bears any resemblance to the real universe, as the summaries in Table 9.5 and 9.6 show.

---

p. The standard measure of power used in radio astronomy is the flux unit, also known as the Jansky. One flux unit, or Jansky, equals 10^{-26} watts per meter squared per cycle per second (or Hertz).

Table 9.5: Evidence refuting long hesitation models

1. The number of galaxies and quasars with red shifts (z) greater than 2.5 is much too large to permit hesitation.

2. Hesitation models with long quasi-static periods are so unstable as to collapse.

3. The observed deceleration parameter, q_o, in the expansion of the universe contradicts the acceleration required by hesitation.

4. Nuclear chronometers and color-luminosity diagrams for star clusters indicate that stars have existed for only a relatively short time (about 20 billion years).

5. Hesitation requires a non-zero value for Λ, yet Λ is the quantity in physics most accurately measured to be zero—less than 10^{-122} in dimensionless units.

6. Disintegration of a primeval atom (a cold big bang, usually designed to support some kind of hesitation model) provides no means to explain the observed abundances of the elements.

7. The cold big bang hesitation models offer no explanation for the observed background radiation, nor do they account for the observed entropy.

Table 9.6: Evidence refuting the steady state model

1. The lack of very old galaxies in the vicinity of our galaxy negates an infinite age for the universe.

2. The lack of very young galaxies in the vicinity of our galaxy negates continual spontaneous creation.

3. The lack of red shifts beyond z = 4 implies a real limit for the universe short of the visual limit expected for an infinite steady state universe.

4. A steady state universe lacks a physical mechanism (such as the primeval explosion) to drive the observed expansion of the universe.

5. The observed microwave background radiation (perfectly explained by the cooling off of the primordial fireball) defies explanation in a steady state universe.

6. The enormous entropy of the universe makes no sense in a steady state system.

7. In a steady state universe, spontaneously generated matter must come into being with a specified ratio of helium to hydrogen, and that ratio must decrease with respect to time in an entirely ad hoc fashion. Instead, the measured helium abundance for the universe has exactly the value that the big bang would predict.

8. The observed abundances of deuterium, light helium, and lithium have no physical explanation in a steady state universe. (Again, a hot big bang precisely predicts them.)

9. Galaxies and quasars at distances so great that we are viewing them from the remote past appear to differ so substantially in character and distribution from nearby, more contemporary, galaxies and quasars as to render steady state models completely implausible.

theological implications

The second and third attempts to avoid the origin of the universe, and with it the originator, have fallen flat. Not only have these "loopholes" been closed, but the "beginning of the present order of Nature" has been unshakably established.

The time between the singularity and the present now has been measured to be about 16 billion years. Volumes of data converge to tell us that, at most, the universe could be 20 billion years old—much too young for evolutionary processes to generate anything akin to life. It seems only rational to conclude that God, not random chance, must be responsible for creating both.

CHAPTER TEN

Oscillating Universe

summary

Given a hot big bang, theoreticians went to work yet again to distance themselves from the dread beginning. They hypothesized a cycle of expansion and contraction for the universe. An infinite number of cycles might remove any need to deal with an ultimate origin for the universe. However, observational evidence suggests that the universe has insufficient mass to force a collapse. Moreover, thermodynamic arguments show that even if the universe were massive enough to collapse, entropy would prevent a rebound. Instead of a bounce, there would be a crunch.

Gribbin's complaint

Research that brought about the demise of the steady state and hesitating universe theories simultaneously strengthened the case for the big bang and, thus, the prospect of an absolute beginning. The implications of such a prospect so disturbed a number of scientists that they turned to the model of early Hindu teachers and Roman atheistic philosophers—the oscillating universe. British physicist John Gribbin voiced the opinion of many:

> The biggest problem with the Big Bang theory of the origin of the Universe is philosophical—perhaps even theological—what was there before the bang? This problem alone was sufficient to give a great initial impetus to the Steady State theory; but with that theory now sadly in conflict with the observations, the best way round this

initial difficulty is provided by a model in which the universe expands from a singularity, collapses back again, and repeats the cycle indefinitely.[1]

de Sitter's proposal

To review from Chapter 9, Friedmann established in 1922 that if the density of the universe were greater than a certain critical value, gravity eventually would halt the expansion and cause the universe to implode back on itself. In 1931 de Sitter leapt from this conclusion to propose, as diagrammed in Figure 10.1, a universe alternately expanding and contracting between a radius of a finite minimum value (possibly zero) and of a finite maximum value.[2] An infinite number of such cycles of expansion and contraction would possibly remove any need to think about an ultimate beginning. De Sitter did admit, however, that the observed density falls far short of Friedmann's critical value.[a]

Tolman's thermodynamic considerations

In that same year, 1931, Richard Tolman ruled out strictly periodic solutions (continuous expansions and contractions between definite minimum and maximum diameters for the universe) to the field equations of general relativity. He demonstrated that irreversible thermodynamic changes take place at a finite rate with continuing increases in entropy.[3-6] In other words, if the universe were going through cycles of expansion and contraction, its maximum diameter would be increasing from cycle to cycle as shown in Figure 10.2. Such oscillation might imply an infinite future for the universe, but only a finite past. Therefore, the universe still must have a beginning.

---

a. At that time the measured density of the universe was almost a hundred times less than what was needed to halt the expansion of the universe.

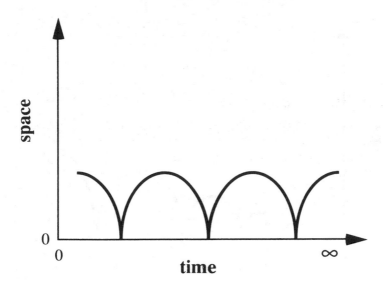

Figure 10.1: The oscillating universe model

In the oscillating model the universe alternates between phases of expansion and contraction. Gravity halts the expansion and generates succeeding phases of contraction. An unknown mechanism somehow bounces the universe from contraction into expansion.

In a continuing effort to circumvent the irksome beginning, several quasi-periodic models were introduced, models that avoided increases in entropy.[3, 4, 7] However, these models were "very highly idealized;" that is, they depended on unrealistic assumptions about the universe (for example, that the universe contains only black body radiation[b]). Also, they ignored a key issue, as conceded by Tolman,[8] the absence of any conceivable physical mechanism to reverse a cosmic contraction. This deficiency remains.

---

b. Radiation is said to be black body if it resembles the emission from an object that has the characteristics of being both a perfect emitter and a perfect absorber of energy.

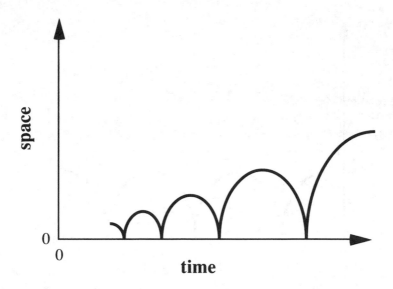

Figure 10.2: The failure of the strictly cyclical universe model
Tolman's thermodynamic principles require that the maximum radius of the universe must increase from cycle to cycle of expansion and contraction. Therefore, the oscillating universe model may predict an infinite future, but only a finite past.

Nevertheless, so strong was the motivation of most physicists and astronomers to escape the beginning that all these difficulties were overlooked or disregarded. Typical was a comment by Tolman himself and Morgan Ward that "it is evident that contraction to zero volume could only be followed by renewed expansion."[8] Not until the 1970's was there an honest exploration of the limitations on oscillation, particularly those imposed by Tolman's line of reasoning. In 1973 Russian theoreticians Igor Novikov and Yakob Zel'dovich demonstrated that there is no possible way (given model characteristics similar to those actually found in our universe) to prevent the maximum radius of a cyclic universe from increasing cycle to cycle.[9] Their point was reiterated in 1975 by

Peter Landsberg and D. Park.[10] In the words of Novikov and Zel'dovich, oscillation provides no escape from an ultimate beginning in the finite past.[11]

missing mass

In 1965 Robert Dicke and his Princeton University colleagues gave the initial interpretation of the discovery of the cosmic background radiation by Bell Telephone scientists Arno Penzias and Robert Wilson.[12, 13] They stated their assumption that the present expansion of the universe is a direct result of the bounce from a previously contracting state. They admitted that "in the framework of conventional theory we cannot understand the origin of matter or of the universe."[14] But, unwilling to concede a solution outside of conventional theory; that is, a supernatural solution, they presumed that the singularity of the universe may be done away with by introducing special anisotropies (properties that vary according to direction) and inhomogeneities (properties that vary randomly from place to place).[c] They stuck to their conclusion:

> ... the matter we see about us now may represent the same baryon [i.e. matter] content of the previous expansion of a closed universe, oscillating for all time. This relieves us of the necessity of understanding the origin of matter at any finite time in the past.[15]

If the origin of the universe were thus safely distant, one might ignore the First Cause and at the same time permit the dice of chance a virtually infinite number of throws.

This line of reasoning became predominant among astrophysicists following the death of the steady state and hesitating universe theories. One of the first to speak along this line was John Gribbin. One of the last was a colleague of Dicke, James Peebles, in 1986:

---

c. It was proven later that no possible combination of anisotropies, inhomogeneities, or nonuniformities could do away with a singular origin for the universe. This work is discussed in the section on singularity theorems in Chapter 11.

This conventional theory [the big bang] has two defects: it fails to explain why the large-scale mass distribution should be so close to uniform and it requires that the expansion can be extrapolated back to a singularity at a definite time in the past.[16]

Of course, this philosophical resistance serves for nought if the universe is open—if the density of the universe falls short of Friedmann's critical value.[d] So, Princeton physicists and astronomers of the 1960 s and 1970 s led an all-out search for what came to be termed the "missing mass" of the the universe.

Back in the 1930 s, Swiss-American physicist Fritz Zwicky had noted a problem in the way galaxy clusters behave. The (estimated) mass of the galaxies we can see is insufficient to hold them together in the clusters where they do, apparently, reside. The force of their random velocities should be more than adequate to disperse the clusters. But the clusters remain.[17, 18] Here was a straw to be grasped! Perhaps matter is hidden, hidden because it is not luminous, not luminous because it is dispersed in relatively small chunks.

Alas, the missing mass hypothesis was weighed in the balance and found somewhat wanting. To be sure, some missing mass was found, in fact, about ten times as much as one would get from adding up all the stars. Richard Gott, James Gunn, David Schramm, and Beatrice Tinsley in 1974 used four independent direct measurements of the density of the universe to determine values (relative to the Friedmann's critical density) of 0.05 ± 0.01.[19] This value included all the baryonic[e] matter within clusters and groups of galaxies. Intercluster matter may exist, but it

d. If the density of the universe falls short of Friedmann's critical value, it is "open." Gravity cannot prevent the universe from expanding forever. If the density exceeds Friedmann's critical value, then gravity eventually will halt the expansion and force a subsequent collapse. Such a universe is "closed." If the universe has a density equal to Friedmann's critical value, it is "flat," expanding forever at a rate just fast enough to prevent collapse.

e. Baryons, also known as nucleons, are the heavier particles, e.g. protons and neutrons, that make up the nucleus of an atom.

would add a negligible amount. Evidence is now accumulating, however, that exotic (i.e. non-baryonic) matter may push the density figure for the universe up to at least 0.2 but probably not more than about 0.4 of Friedmann's critical value.[20 - 21] Even Peebles, who was one of the strongest advocates for a closed universe, now concedes that the density of the universe is only three-tenths of Friedmann's critical value.[22] Recent measurements all favor an open, rather than a closed, universe.[23 - 27]

inflationary universe model

A new version of the big bang model—a model called the inflationary universe—provides a compelling argument as to why the density of the universe should exactly equal Friedmann's critical value. Invented by Alan Guth in 1980,[28] the inflationary model answers most of the previously unanswered questions of big bang cosmology.

In the standard big bang model, the universe expands smoothly and adiabatically[f] from the beginning onward. In the inflationary model there is a very brief departure from adiabatic expansion. A much faster, exponential expansion occurs between about 10^{-35} and about 10^{-33} seconds after the beginning.[g]

Over large scale distances the universe exhibits a high degree of homogeneity and isotropy.[h] These characteristics imply that all regions in the universe must have remained causally connected (what happens in one region affects the adjacent regions) to one another throughout their history. The problem with strict adiabatic expansion is that the present universe is far too big for all its regions to have been causally connected at a time near the origin.

---

f. Under adiabatic expansion the temperature will drop due to expansion alone without loss of heat from the system.

g. In some inflationary models periods of exponential expansion also take place before 10^{-35} seconds.[29]

h. An isotropic universe maintains the same physical properties regardless of the direction of measurement.

Now, a mechanism that stops the adiabatic expansion and blows up a small, causally connected region into something the size of the observable universe will solve the problem. Moreover, an abrupt increase in the radius of a causally connected region will:

a) decrease radically its curvature, thus explaining why the universe is so nearly flat, i.e. with a density so close to Friedmann's critical value, and

b) dilute topological defects such as magnetic monopoles and domain walls,[i] thereby explaining why such phenomena have never been observed.

Astrophysicists agree that a model that explains so much must contain a significant germ of truth. Thus, when some of the more successful inflationary models predict perfect flatness for the universe, their predictions are taken seriously.[j] A perfectly flat universe expands forever, without collapse, without oscillation.

impossibility of a bounce

While it has long been acknowledged that no known physical mechanism can ever reverse (rebound) a cosmic contraction, more fundamental limitations on a "bounce" have recently been discovered. Novikov and Zel'dovich have pointed out that uniform isotropic compression

---

i. A magnetic monopole is a particle carrying an isolated north or south magnetic pole. It is very massive. Hence, it has the capacity to release enormous amounts of energy. Magnetic monopoles form at point defects in the surface topology of the very early universe. Strings are line defects, and domain walls are plane defects. They are orders of magnitude more massive again than magnetic monopoles.

j. Because there is not enough ordinary matter (i.e. baryons) to gain Friedmann's critical density value, the "missing" mass would need to be made up of exotic matter such as massive neutrinos.[25] Even with the addition of exotic matter, observational constraints now limit the density of the universe to less than half the critical density. As a result, inflationary models with densities slightly less than critical (and therefore open) are being designed.[21, 27]

becomes violently unstable near the end of the collapse phase, and the collapsing medium breaks up into fragments.[30] This problem along with some straightforward thermodynamics, recognized in the last couple of years, rule out any possibility for a bouncing universe.[31, 32]

As noted earlier, the universe, with a specific entropy of about a billion, ranks as the most entropic phenomenon known. Thus, even if the universe contained sufficient mass to force an eventual collapse, that collapse would *not* produce a bounce. Far too much of the energy of the universe is dissipated in unreclaimable form to fuel a bounce. Like a lump of wet clay falling on a carpet, the universe, if it did collapse, would go "splat."

summary of evidence against oscillation

Since 1984 the accumulation of evidence has ruled out the oscillating universe model. To review briefly, that evidence includes the following:

1. Cyclical expansion and contraction of the universe, if such did take place, would result in an ever-increasing radius, traceable backward to a first cycle.

2. The observed density of the universe appears to be at most only one-half of what is needed to force a collapse.

3. The density implied by the inflationary model will not force a collapse.

4. No physical mechanism is known that could realistically be expected to reverse a cosmic contraction.

5. Isotropic compression becomes violently unstable near the end of the collapse phase.

6. If the universe were to collapse, a bounce would be impossible because the universe is so entropic.

Attempts by Robert Dicke, John Gribbin, James Peebles, and others to use oscillation to avoid a theistic beginning for the universe all fail.

CHAPTER ELEVEN

Transcendence and Quantum Gravity

summary

One theorem of general relativity proves that space and time share a common origin with the universe. This theorem effectively eliminates any possibility for an infinite universe, and yields a powerful argument for the biblical statement about creation. However, there remains a tiny instant just after the beginning of the universe about which science has little or no knowledge. Some physicists have waxed metaphysical about "quantum gravity" during this era. Though most, through adherence to the "beauty principle," remain reconciled with the concept (at least) of the biblical Creator, a few seize upon our ignorance of that moment to propose bizarre possibilities. Their expressed motive is to push the Creator into the remote distance.

With the defeat of the static, hesitation, steady state, and oscillation models for the universe, no observationally testable alternative remained (by 1984) to make the universe infinitely old and thereby to save evolutionism.[a]

---

a. The basic definition of evolution is change taking place through time. As such, the universe clearly has evolved. Evolutionism, however, attributes all change in the universe, both organic and inorganic, to natural processes alone, i.e. without input from a divine designer.

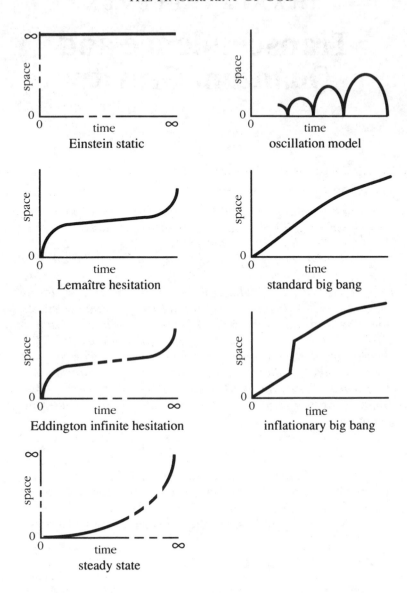

Figure 11.1: Seven types of testable models for the universe.

Observations have ruled out all but the big bang models.

The observations only allowed the standard big bang[b] [1, 2, 3] and the inflationary big bang models,[c] [4, 5, 6] both of which established a finite age for the universe. (The seven basic classes of testable models for the universe are diagrammed in Figure 11.1.) A more fundamental limitation on evolutionism began to emerge, however, in the late 1960 s.

singularity theorem

According to the standard expanding universe model, the universe begins in a state of infinite density and infinite temperature—the big bang singularity. Richard Tolman and others, from the 1930 s onward, had hoped that this singularity was merely an artifact from the assumption that the universe was highly symmetric.[7] Surely in a physically realistic universe the singularity would disappear. Not so; the evidence for a "singular" past only compounded. Calculations based on all manner of asymmetries, distortions, lumps, and rotations not only predicted that the singularity would remain, but that it would occur even more recently than in the perfectly symmetric case.[8]

To some, the singularity presented an uncomfortable "interface between the natural and the supernatural,"[9] even "monstrously" so.[10] Therefore, they persisted in asking, "Is the singularity avoidable?"

---

b. In the standard big bang model all matter, energy, space, and time expands adiabatically (without gain or loss of total heat) according to the equations of general relativity from an initial state of infinite density, temperature, and pressure.

c. In the inflationary big bang model the universe expands in the same fashion as the standard big bang model except that for a brief period between 10^{-43} and 10^{-34} seconds after the creation event the universe experiences a much more rapid exponential expansion.

Three British astrophysicists, Roger Penrose, Stephen Hawking, and George Ellis, sought to answer this question. Employing no assumptions that cannot be tested by observations, they demonstrated that under very general conditions every solution to the equations of general relativity guarantees the existence of a singular boundary for space and time in the past—a result now known as the "singularity theorem."[11, 12] Specifically, a universe that is expanding, filled with matter and energy, and obeying any physically acceptable equation of state must have been singular in the past, regardless of any lack of symmetry today.

observational constraints

Four basic assumptions underlie the singularity theorem. First, gravity is always attractive. Second, time moves forward only, not backward. Third, the universe contains enough matter to generate at least one black hole. Fourth, the equations of general relativity accurately describe the universe.[d]

The first two assumptions appear straightforward. Indeed, their overthrow would admittedly be much more monstrous than the singularity.[13] The third was the subject of a paper by Ellis and Hawking. In it they determined that the gravitational attraction exerted by the microwave background radiation, by itself, is always sufficient to create a "trapped" region, a black hole out of which not even light can escape the tug of gravity.[11]

---

d. The specific conditions of the singularity theorem are:
   1. The spacetime manifold for our universe satisfies the equations of general relativity.
   2. Timetravel into the past is impossible.
   3. Principle of causality is not violated (no closed timelike curves).
   4. Mass density and pressure of matter never becomes negative.
   5. There is enough matter present to generate a trapped surface.
   6. The spacetime manifold is not too highly symmetric.

This should have settled the matter. But, at the time Penrose, Hawking, and Ellis were developing their theorem (1967-1970), general relativity was verified only to one or two decimal places. Thus, in the 1960s and 1970s a few theoreticians designed cosmological models based on slight departures from general relativity.[14 - 16] This work has been abandoned, however, since sophisticated experiments have verified general relativity to three, four, and even five places of the decimal (see the list of experiments and references in Table 5.1).

origin of space and time

From Einstein's work on general relativity came the recognition that there must be an origin for matter and energy. From Penrose, Hawking, and Ellis' work came the acknowledgment that there must be an origin for space and time, too.[17]

With the knowledge that time has a beginning, and a relatively recent beginning, at that, all age-lengthening attempts to push away the creation event, and thus the Creator, become absurd. Moreover, the common origin of matter, energy, space, and time proves that the act(s) of creation must transcend the dimensions and substance of the the universe—a powerful argument for the biblical doctrine of a transcendent Creator.

reaction to the singularity

While the evidence for a transcendent creation event is receiving general acceptance throughout the physical science community, there are some notable holdouts. The American theoretician, Heinz Pagels,[e] for one, refuses to acknowledge that physical singularities can ever exist. He says, "The appearance of such a singularity is a good reason for rejecting the standard model of the very origin of the universe altogether."[18] While admitting that

---

e. Pagels was killed in a mountaineering accident in 1988.

Einstein's equations of general relativity, along with observationally verified conditions, do require an inevitable singularity, he nonetheless feels that in the region of ignorance at the beginning of time a loophole *must* exist. Of the Penrose-Hawking-Ellis theorem Pagels says "... their work did not prove that these extreme conditions were really present at the beginning of time."[18]

Pagels' point is that astrophysicists have a good understanding of the development of the universe only as far back as 10^{-34} seconds after the (apparent) singular creation event. He is not demeaning a phenomenal achievement, but simply points out that there still remains a tiny interval about which science has little knowledge.

It is in that moment before the universe is 10^{-34} seconds old that the standard and inflationary big bang models diverge. If the inflationary scenario is correct, then the inflation would have washed out any preinflationary features of the universe. No observational clues as to what happened before 10^{-34} seconds would remain.

Using the "beauty principle" of physics[f] it may be possible to discern a few properties of the universe back to 10^{-43} seconds. Before that, however, there is no tool, observational or theoretical, to test what occurred. Nor is there any such tool on the horizon. A particle accelerator more than ten trillion miles long would be needed to probe the era before 10^{-34} seconds. At 10^{-43} seconds, the strength of the gravitational force should be comparable to that of the strong nuclear force. Hence, gravity may be modified by quantum mechanics. Here the space-time geometry of the universe could decompose into what physicists call a "space-time foam." Exactly what or how much happens, though, remains pure speculation.

---

f. The beauty principle is the presupposition that the correct description of nature is that which manifests the greatest degree of simplicity, beauty, elegance, and consistency. So far this principle has been an unerring guide to new insights in theoretical physics. It also is a statement about who or what created the universe.

Astrophysicists, nevertheless, have eagerly leaped into that narrow abyss. The period of ignorance before 10^{-43} seconds has given rise to a veritable explosion of "wild ideas" about the origin of the universe.

As far back as 1973, Ed Tryon suggested that a quantum mechanical fluctuation in "the vacuum" created the universe.[19] Later, he was joined by several other American and Russian theoreticians,[20 - 24] all of whom have posited that by the laws of physics "nothing is unstable."[g] While one of this group's members, the inventor of the inflationary big bang model, Alan Guth, concedes that "such ideas are speculation squared," all of their models do circumvent the big bang singularity. They do not, however, circumvent the beginning of space-time-matter-energy. Thus, agreement with the biblical doctrine of creation still stands.

One of the most elegant vacuum fluctuation models was published in 1984 when Steven Hawking teamed up with American physicist James Hartle.[25, 26] They say that just as a hydrogen atom can be described by a quantum mechanical wave function, so can the universe be described. By such means they show that the singularity disappears, and yet the entire universe still pops into existence at the beginning of time. As Pagels puts it:

> This unthinkable void converts itself into the plenum of existence—a necessary consequence of physical laws. Where are these laws written into that void? What "tells" the void that it is pregnant with a possible universe? It would seem that even the void is subject to law, a logic that exists prior to space and time.[27]

Once again, the biblical doctrine of creation is deduced.

---

g. In quantum theory the Heisenberg uncertainty principle permits random fluctuations in empty space to produce real particles (providing such particles transform back into nothing before any observer can detect their existence). Hence, some theorists suppose that, in the yet-to-be (or never-to-be) discovered quantum gravity theory, space-time itself may arise from a random fluctuation in the primordial nothingness.

Later, in 1988, Hawking reformulated his escape from the singularity in his popular book *A Brief History of Time:*

If the universe really is in such a quantum state, there would be no singularities in the history of the universe in imaginary time. ... The universe could be finite in imaginary time but without boundaries or singularities. When one goes back to the real time in which we live, however, there will still appear to be singularities. ... Only if [we] lived in imaginary time would [we] encounter no singularities. ... In real time, the universe has a beginning and an end at singularities that form a boundary to space-time and at which the laws of science break down.[28]

In other words, God, who according to the Bible transcends "real time,"[29] would not be confined to boundaries and singularities, but human beings and the physical universe, both of which are limited to real time, would be so confined. Hence, Hawking's famous query notwithstanding ("What place, then, for a creator?"[30]), there is still no escape from the biblical doctrine of creation.[h]

reaction to the beginning of time

Lately, quantum mechanical musings have led to a rejection of any kind of recent beginning. The American astrophysicist Richard Gott and Belgium's François Englert and his colleagues have attempted to distance themselves from the dread singularity by designing models that put it forever out of reach.

In the model devised by Englert, Brout, Gunzig, and Spindel,[33, 34] the universe begins with zero mass but with quantum mechanics supposedly in operation. An

---

h. Hawking's stated goal is "a complete understanding of everything."[31] Since the existence of the God of the Bible and/or singularities would guarantee that his goal would never be reached, he seeks to deny both. Ironically, his goal was proven mathematically impossible by Kurt Gödel in 1930. According to Gödel's incompleteness theorem, with incomplete information about a system, one cannot prove a necessarily true theorem (i.e. a one and only one description) about that system.[32]

inevitable quantum mechanical fluctuation induces an expansion of space which in their theory produces a small quantity of matter. This newly created matter then induces a further expansion of space which produces yet more matter. Eventually, a density equivalent to that at the start of the inflationary big bang model is reached, at which point matter production stops and the universe continues to develop according to the inflationary model. According to the Englert et al model, it is possible that the time required for the universe to grow from a zero mass state to that of the inflationary big bang approaches infinity, and in this nearly infinite time the singularity is thought to be pushed beyond philosophical consideration.

In Gott's model, the density of the universe remains "on hold" from infinity-past through the beginning of the inflationary period at 10^{-43} seconds.[35] A comparison between Gott's model, the Englert et al model, and the big bang models is given in Figure 11.2. Gott's model is really a sophisticated revival of de Sitter's static model. The "outside" infinitely old and large universe contains nothing but radiation at extremely high but finite and constant temperature and pressure. The universe is merely an expanding bubble (and hence cooler) within the much larger de Sitter space. The 3°K black body background radiation rather than arising from the cooling off of the big bang, simply reflects conditions in the outside universe.

To pull this off, Gott postulates special conditions and a large Λ (Einstein's cosmological constant) that decays to zero by 10^{-43} seconds after the "apparent" creation event. Gott sets up his model in such a way as to guarantee that there never will be any observational falsification or verification. To quote him,

> An infinite amount of information is lost about what happens beyond the horizon [before 10^{-43} seconds]. The existence of an event horizon means that there is a region of which we can never have any knowledge.[36]

115

Behind this event horizon Gott sees the possibility of an infinite number of universes. He continues,

> The ability to make an infinite number of universes in the region goes with the infinite loss of information about this region suggested by the area of the event horizon.[36]

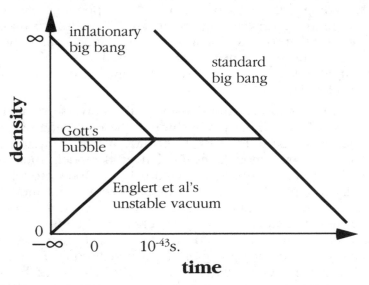

Figure 11.2: Early era speculations

With no possibility in sight for testing the characteristics of the universe before 10^{-43} seconds after its "beginning," Richard Gott, François Englert, and Englert's colleagues feel free to speculate on bizarre "possibilities" for that era. The conditions their models postulate would not only yield significant departures from the big bang models but would also elude the singularity so as to push away into the infinite past the beginning of space-time-matter-energy.

In this proposed "infinite number of universes" some non-theists see an opportunity to replace God with chance, or, more specifically, with random fluctuations of

Gott's primeval radiation field. They propose that the universe was created by the impersonal force of the de Sitter radiation field. But, inevitably, one must have a personal transcendent Creator to explain where the de Sitter force came from. Moreover, if the universe had zero information content before 10^{-43} seconds, where did it acquire its subsequent high information state without the input of an intelligent, personal, Creator?

While the beauty principle does guide one to a biblical conclusion about creation, departures from the principle, of course, can lead to some distancing from the Creator. But, that is all. The non-theists' speculations on that moment of the unknown resembles ancient philosophers' arguments for the non-existence of their chairs—the very ones on which they sat—based on the fact that not *everything* about the chairs was known to them.

reaction to the transcendent Creator

British astrophysicist and science popularizer Paul Davies, in his book *God and the New Physics,* used the beginning of space-time to argue against God's involvement in creating the universe. Davies equated the time dimension of this universe with all cause-and-effect relationships. All cause-and-effect phenomena are time bound, he says. And since God could only create through cause-and-effect, Davies used the evidence for the origin of time to argue against God's agency in creating the universe.[37] Then, noting that virtual particles can pop into existence from nothingness through quantum tunneling,[i] he employed the new grand unified theories to suggest that in the same manner the whole universe popped into existence.

---

i. Quantum tunneling is the process by which quantum particles penetrate barriers that are insurmountable to classical objects.

Davies never overtly denied the existence of God. But, he certainly suggested a reshaping of our concept of Him. Apparently, Davies was unaware that the Bible specifically states that God acted, that He caused effects, before the beginning of time.[29] The Bible also describes the existence of dimensions beyond those that we experience (one time and three space) and to which our universe is confined. To say that God cannot act beyond the dimensions of the universe is to neglect the possibility of extra dimensions. Ironically, the theory of superstrings, now very popular with theoretical physicists, is founded upon the evidence for dimensions beyond the four we experience.[38]

While God is not limited, quantum mechanical processes are. Quantum mechanics is founded on the concept that there are finite probabilities for quantum events to take place within certain time intervals. The greater the interval of time, the greater the probability. But, without time, no quantum event is possible.[j] Therefore, the origin of time (and space, matter, and energy) eliminates quantum tunneling as "Creator."

To Paul Davies' credit, he has shown a willingness to keep searching, to keep developing new hypotheses. He recently argued that the laws of physics "seem themselves to be the product of exceedingly ingenious design," and that "the universe must have a purpose."[39]

j. Since we lack knowledge about everything before 10^{-43} seconds, there necessarily exists the *possibility* that the relationship between time and the probability for certain quantum events may break down in that interval.

CHAPTER TWELVE

Design and the Anthropic Principle

summary

Human existence is possible because the constants of physics and the parameters of the universe and Earth lie within certain highly restricted ranges. Some interpret these amazing "coincidences" as proof that man somehow designs the universe. Drawing an illogical parallel with delayed-choice experiments in quantum mechanics, they say that human observations influence the design of the universe, now, and even back to the beginning. Such versions of the "anthropic principle" reflect current philosophical leanings towards the deification of man. No one has produced evidence to support the notion that man's present acts can influence the past. Analogies with quantum mechanics break down on this point. The "coincidental" values of the constants of physics and the parameters of the universe point, rather, to a designer who transcends the dimensions and limits of the physical universe.

cosmic connection

Now that limits and parameters for the universe can be calculated—some, directly measured—astronomers and physicists have begun to see a connection between these factors and the existence of life. They have found it impossible to hypothesize a universe containing life in which any one of the fundamental constants of physics or any of the several parameters of the universe is more than slightly different in one way or another.

From this recognition arises the *anthropic principle*, which says that everything about the universe tends toward man, toward making life possible and sustaining it. The first popularizer of the principle, American physicist John Wheeler, describes it in this way: "A life-giving factor lies at the centre of the whole machinery and design of the world."[1]

Of course, design in the natural world has been acknowledged since the beginning of recorded history. Divine design is the message of each of the several hundred creation accounts that form the basis of the world's religions.[2, 3] The idea that the natural world was designed especially for mankind is the very bedrock of the Judaic, Greek, and Christian world-views. Western philosophers of the post-Roman era went so far as to formalize a discipline called *teleology*—the study of the evidence for overall design and purpose in nature. Teleology attracted such luminaries as Augustine, Maimonides, Aquinas, Newton, and Paley, all of whom gave it much of their life's work.

Dirac and Dicke's coincidences

One of the first to recognize that design also may apply to the gross features of the universe was American physicist Robert Dicke. In 1937, British physicist Paul Dirac had noted that the number of baryons (basically protons plus neutrons) in the universe (10^{80}) is almost exactly equal to the inverse square of the gravitational constant (10^{40}) and to the square of the age of the universe (10^{40}).[a, 4] In 1961 Dicke discerned that these

---

a. The gravitational constant and age of the universe are expressed, here, not in culture-bound units of force or time, but in dimensionless units, i.e. as ratios of the smallest meaningful physical measurements (e.g. the time for light to traverse the radius of an electron). Dirac's gravitational constant = $2\pi Gm_p^2/hc$ while his age for the universe = $2\pi Tm_p c/h$ where m_p is the mass of some elementary particle, c the velocity of light, h Planck's constant, G the gravitational constant, and T the Hubble age of the universe.

relationships would imply a narrow window of time in the development of the universe during which life could exist.[5] Stars of the right type for sustaining planets capable of supporting life can occur only during a certain age range for the universe. Similarly, stars of the right type can form only within a narrow range of values for the gravitational constant (as explained below).

the universe as a fit habitat

In recent years these and other parameters for the universe have been more sharply defined and analyzed. In the process, nearly two dozen "coincidences" indicating design have been acknowledged, including the following:

1. The **gravitational coupling constant** (the force of gravity) determines what kinds of stars are possible in the universe. If the gravitational force were slightly stronger, star formation would proceed more efficiently and all stars would be more massive than our sun by at least 1.4 times. These large stars are important in that they alone manufacture elements heavier than iron, and they alone disperse elements heavier than beryllium to the interstellar medium. Such elements are essential for the formation of planets as well as of living things in any form. However, these stars burn too rapidly and too inconstantly to maintain life-supporting conditions on surrounding planets. Stars as small as our sun are necessary for that.

On the other hand, if the gravitational force were slightly weaker, all stars would have less than 0.8 times the mass of the sun. Though such stars burn long enough and evenly enough to maintain life-supporting planets, there would be no heavy elements for building such planets or life, itself.

2. The **strong nuclear force coupling constant** holds together the particles in the nucleus of an atom. If the strong nuclear force were slightly weaker, multi-proton nuclei would not hold together. Hydrogen would be the only element in the universe.

If this force were slightly stronger, nuclear particles would tend to bond together more frequently and more firmly. Not only would hydrogen (a bachelor nuclear particle) be rare in the universe, but the supply of the various life-essential elements heavier than iron (elements resulting from the fission of very heavy elements) would be insufficient. Either way, life would be impossible.[b]

3. The **weak nuclear force coupling constant** affects the behavior of leptons. Leptons form a whole class of elementary particles (e.g. neutrinos, electrons, and photons) that do not participate in strong nuclear reactions. The most familiar weak interaction effect is radioactivity, in particular, the beta decay reaction:

neutron → proton + electron + neutrino.

The availability of neutrons as the universe cools through temperatures appropriate for nuclear fusion determines the amount of helium produced during the first few minutes of the big bang. If the weak nuclear force coupling constant were slightly larger, neutrons would decay more readily, and therefore would be less available. Hence, little or no helium would be produced from the big bang. Without the necessary helium, heavy elements sufficient for the construction of life would not be made by the nuclear furnaces inside stars. On the other hand, if this constant were slightly smaller, the big bang would burn most or all of the hydrogen into helium, with a subsequent over-abundance of heavy elements made by stars, and again life would not be possible.

A second, possibly tighter, restriction on the value of the weak nuclear force comes from its effect on neutrinos. If the weak nuclear force were smaller, neutrinos would quietly escape during a supernova explosion, failing to interact sufficiently with the the outer layers of the star, and thus preventing significant expulsion of heavy ele-

b. The strong nuclear force is actually much more delicately balanced. An increase as small as two percent means that protons would never form from quarks (particles that form the building blocks of baryons and mesons). A similar decrease means that certain heavy elements essential for life would be unstable.

ments. Whereas, if the weak nuclear force were larger, neutrinos would be trapped inside the cores of supernovae and again would be unable to facilitate the expulsion of the heavy elements which are the building blocks for life.

4. The **electromagnetic coupling constant** binds electrons to protons in atoms. The characteristics of the orbits of electrons about atomic nuclei determines to what degree atoms will bond together to form molecules. If the electromagnetic coupling constant were slightly smaller, few electrons would be held in orbits about nuclei. If it were slightly larger, an atom could not "share" an electron orbit with other atoms. Either way, the necessary molecules for life would not exist.

5. The **ratio of protons to electrons** establishes the role of gravity relative to electromagnetism. When the universe was less than a second old, anti-protons quickly annihilated all their partner protons, and just a few protons were left. The same thing happened with electrons and positrons (anti-electrons). Amazingly, the protons and electrons that remained were equivalent in number to better than one part in 10^{37}. Had the balance been any different, electromagnetism would have so dominated gravity that galaxies, stars, and planets never could have formed.

6. The **ratio of electron to proton mass** also determines the characteristics of the orbits of electrons about nuclei. A proton is 1836 times more massive than an electron. If the electron to proton mass ratio were much larger or smaller, again, the necessary molecules would not form, and life would be impossible.

7. The **age of the universe** governs what kinds of stars exist. It took about 2 billion years for the first stars to form. It took another 10 to 12 billion years for supernovae to spew out enough heavy elements to make possible stars like our sun, stars capable of spawning rocky planets. Yet another few billion years was necessary for solar-type stars to stabilize sufficiently to support advanced life on any planet. Hence, if the universe were just a couple of billion years younger, no environment suitable for life would exist. However, if the universe were 10 (or more) billion years older than it is, there would be no solar-type stars in a stable burning phase in the right part of a galaxy. In

other words, the window of time during which life is possible in the universe is relatively narrow.

8. The **expansion rate of the universe** determines what kinds of stars, if any, form in the universe. If the rate of expansion were slightly slower, the whole universe would have recollapsed before any solar-type stars could have settled into a stable burning phase. If the universe were expanding slightly more rapidly, no galaxies (and hence no stars) would have condensed from the general expansion. How critical is this expansion rate? According to Alan Guth,[6] it must be fine-tuned to an accuracy of one part in 10^{55}. Guth, however, suggests that his inflationary model, given certain values for the four fundamental forces of physics, may provide a natural explanation for the critical expansion rate.

9. The **entropy level of the universe** affects the degree to which massive systems (e.g. galaxies and stars) condense. The ratio of photons to baryons tells us how entropic our universe is. That ratio is about a billion to one. Thus, we can say that the universe is extremely entropic, i.e. a very efficient radiator and a very poor engine. If the entropy level for the universe were slightly larger, no galactic systems would form (and therefore no stars). If the entropy level were slightly smaller, the galactic systems that formed would effectively trap radiation and prevent any fragmentation of the systems into stars. Either way, the universe would be devoid of stars and, thus, of life. (Some models for the universe relate this coincidence to a dependence of entropy upon the gravitational coupling constant.[7, 8])

10. The **mass of the universe** (actually mass + energy, since $E = mc^2$) determines how much nuclear burning takes place as the universe cools from the hot big bang. If the mass were slightly larger, too much deuterium (hydrogen atoms with nuclei containing both a proton and a neutron) would form during the cooling of the big bang. Deuterium is a powerful catalyst for subsequent nuclear burning in stars. This extra deuterium would cause stars to burn too rapidly to sustain life on any possible planet.

On the other hand, if the mass of the universe were slightly smaller, no helium would be generated during the cooling of the big bang. Without helium, stars cannot produce the heavy elements necessary for life. If the universe were any smaller (or larger), not even one planet like the earth would be possible.

11. The **uniformity of the universe** determines its stellar components. Our universe has a high degree of uniformity. Such uniformity is considered to arise most probably from a brief period of inflationary expansion near the time of the origin of the universe. If the inflation (or some other mechanism) had not smoothed the universe to the degree we see, the universe would have developed into a plethora of black holes separated by virtually empty space.

On the other hand, if the universe were smoother, the condensations necessary to form stars, star clusters, and galaxies would never have come to exist. Either way, the resultant universe would be incapable of supporting life.

12. The **stability of the proton** affects the quantity of matter in the universe and the radiation level (in the range that would affect higher life forms). Each proton contains three quarks. Through the agency of other particles (called bosons), quarks decay into antiquarks, pions, and positrons. Currently in our universe this decay process occurs on the average of only once per proton per 10^{32} years.[c] If that rate were greater, the biological consequences for large animals and man would be catastrophic, for the proton decays would deliver lethal doses of radiation.

On the other hand, if the proton were more stable (less easily formed and less likely to decay), less matter would have emerged from events occurring in the first split second of the universe's existence. There would be insufficient matter in the universe for life to be possible.

13. The **fine structure constants** relate to each of the four fundamental forces—gravitational, strong nuclear, weak nuclear, and electromagnetic. Compared to the

---

c. Direct observations of proton decay have yet to be confirmed. Experiments simply reveal that the average proton lifetime must exceed 10^{32} years.[9] However, according to some grand unified theories (but not all), if the average proton lifetime were to exceed about 10^{34} years, there would be no physical means for generating matter in the universe.

coupling constants, the fine structure constants typically yield stricter design constraints for the universe. For example, the electromagnetic fine structure constant affects the opacity of stellar material. (Opacity is the degree to which a material permits radiant energy to pass through.) In star formation, gravity pulls material together while thermal motions tend to pull it apart. An increase in the opacity will limit the effect of thermal motions. Hence, smaller clumps of material will be able to overcome the resistance of the thermal motions. If the electromagnetic fine structure constant were slightly larger, all the stars would be less than 0.7 times the mass of the sun. If the electromagnetic fine structure constant were slightly smaller, all the stars would be more than 1.8 times the mass of the sun.

14. The **velocity of light** can be expressed as a function of any one of the fundamental forces of physics or as a function of one of the fine structure constants. Any real changes in the velocity (now *defined* to be 299,792,458 m/s) of light would alter all of these constants. Thus, the slightest variation in the velocity of light, up or down, would negate the possibility for life in the universe.

15. The ^{8}Be, ^{12}C, and ^{16}O **nuclear energy levels** affect the manufacture and abundances of elements essential to life. Atomic nuclei exist in various discrete energy levels. A transition from one level to another occurs through the emission or capture of a photon that possesses precisely the energy difference between the two levels. The first coincidence here is that ^{8}Be decays in just 10^{-15} seconds. Because ^{8}Be is so highly unstable, it slows down the fusion process. If it were more stable, fusion of heavier elements would proceed so readily that catastrophic stellar explosions would result. Such explosions would prevent the formation of many heavy elements essential for life. On the other hand, if ^{8}Be were even more unstable, element production beyond ^{8}Be would not occur.

The second coincidence is that ^{12}C happens to have a nuclear energy level very slightly above the sum of the energy levels for ^{8}Be and ^{4}He. Anything other than this precise nuclear energy level for ^{12}C would guarantee insufficient carbon production for life. The third coincidence is that ^{16}O has the right nuclear energy level both to prevent all the carbon from turning into oxygen and to facilitate sufficient production of ^{16}O for life.

In summary, the ground state energies for ^4He, ^8Be, ^{12}C, and ^{16}O could not be higher or lower with respect to each other by more than four percent without yielding a universe with insufficient oxygen or carbon for any kind of life.[10] Fred Hoyle, who discovered these coincidences in 1953, concluded that "a superintellect has monkeyed with physics, as well as with chemistry and biology."[11]

16. The **distance between stars** affects the orbits and even the existence of planets. The average distance between stars in our part of the galaxy is about 30 trillion miles. If this distance were slightly smaller, gravitational interaction among stars would destabilize planetary orbits. This destabilization would create extreme temperature variations on the planets. If the distance were slightly greater, heavy element debris thrown out by supernovae would be so thinly distributed that rocky planets like earth would never form. The average distance between stars is just right to make possible a planetary system such as our own.

17. The **rate of luminosity increase for stars** affects the temperature conditions on encircling planets. Small stars, like the sun, settle into stable burning once the hydrogen fusion process ignites within their core. However, during this stable phase such stars undergo a very gradual increase in their luminosity. This gradual increase is perfectly suitable for the gradual introduction of life forms, in a sequence from primitive to advanced, upon a planet. (The start date for the first life form and the rate of introduction of subsequent life forms are both, of course, highly critical.) If the rate of luminosity increase were slightly greater, a runaway green house effect[d] would be felt sometime

---

d. An example of the greenhouse effect is a car parked in the sun. Visible light from the sun passes through the car's windows, is absorbed by the interior, and reradiated as infrared light. But, the windows will not permit the passage of infrared radiation. Hence, heat accumulates in the car. Carbon dioxide in the atmosphere works like the car's windows. The early earth's atmosphere had much more carbon dioxide. However, the first plants extracted this carbon dioxide and released oxygen. Hence, the increase in the sun's luminosity was balanced by the decrease in the greenhouse effect caused by the diminished amount of carbon dioxide.

between the introduction of the primitive life forms and the introduction of the advanced life forms. If the rate of increase were slightly smaller, a runaway freezing[e] of the oceans and lakes would occur. Either way, the planet's temperature would become too extreme for advanced life or even for the long-term survival of primitive life.

This list of sensitive constants is by no means complete. And yet it demonstrates why a growing number of physicists and astronomers have been considering the possibility that the universe was not only divinely caused but also divinely designed. American astronomer George Greenstein expresses his thoughts on the subject:

> As we survey all the evidence, the thought insistently arises that some supernatural agency—or, rather, Agency—must be involved. Is it possible that suddenly, without intending to, we have stumbled upon scientific proof of the existence of a Supreme Being? Was it God who stepped in and so providentially crafted the cosmos for our benefit?[12, f]

the earth as a fit habitat

It is not just the universe that bears evidence for design. The earth itself reveals such evidence. Frank Drake, Carl Sagan, and Iosef Shklovsky were among the first astronomers to concede this point in attempting to estimate the number of planets (in the universe) with environments favorable for life support. In the early 1960s they recognized that a certain kind of star with a planet just the right distance from that star would provide the necessary conditions for life.[13] On this basis they made optimistic estimates for the probability of finding

---

e. Runaway freezing would occur because snow and ice reflect better than other materials on the earth. Less solar energy is absorbed, thus the surface temperature decreases. In turn, more snow and ice forms.

f. To be fair, George Greenstein rejects biblical theism as an answer to his query. He embraces a pantheistic solution.

life elsewhere in the universe. Shklovsky and Sagan, for example, claimed that 0.001 percent of all stars could have a planet capable of supporting advanced life.[14]

While their analysis was a step in the right direction, it overestimated the range of permissible star types and the range of permissible planetary distances. It also ignored *many* other significant factors. Some sample parameters sensitive for the support of life are listed in Table 12.1.

Table 12.1: Evidence for the design of the sun-earth-moon system[15 - 32]

The following parameters cannot exceed certain limits without disturbing a planet's capacity to support life. Some of these parameters are more narrowly confining than others. For example, the first parameter would eliminate only sixty percent of the stars from candidacy for life-supporting systems, whereas parameters 5, 7, and 8 would each eliminate more than ninety-nine in one hundred star-planet systems. Not only must the parameters for life-support fall within a certain restrictive range, but they must remain relatively constant over time. Several, such as parameters 14 through 20, are subject to potentially catastrophic fluctuation. In addition to the parameters listed here, there are others, such as the eccentricity of a planet's orbit, that have an upper (or a lower) limit only.

1. number of stars in the planetary system

    if more than one: tidal interactions would disrupt planetary orbits.

    if less than one: heat produced would be insufficient for life.

2. parent star birth date

    if more recent: star would not yet have reached stable burning phase.

    if less recent: stellar system would not yet contain enough heavy elements.

3. parent star age

    if older: luminosity of star would change too quickly.

    if younger: luminosity of star would change too quickly.

4. parent star distance from center of galaxy

   if farther: quantity of heavy elements would be insufficient to make rocky planets.

   if closer: stellar density and radiation would be too great.

5. parent star mass

   if greater: luminosity of star would change too quickly; star would burn too rapidly.

   if less: range of distances appropriate for life would be too narrow; tidal forces would disrupt the rotational period for a planet of the right distance; uv radiation would be inadequate for plants to make sugars and oxygen.

6. parent star color

   if redder: photosynthetic response would be insufficient.

   if bluer: photosynthetic response would be insufficient.

7. surface gravity

   if stronger: atmosphere would retain too much ammonia and methane.

   if weaker: planet's atmosphere would lose too much water.

8. distance from parent star

   if farther: planet would be too cool for a stable water cycle.

   if closer: planet would be too warm for a stable water cycle.

9. axial tilt

   if greater: surface temperature differences would be too great.

   if less: surface temperature differences would be too great.

10. rotation period

    if longer: diurnal temperature differences would be too great.

    if shorter: atmospheric wind velocities would be too great.

11. gravitational interaction with a moon

    if greater: tidal effects on the oceans, atmosphere, and rotational period would be too severe.

    if less: orbital obliquity changes would cause climatic instabilities.

12. magnetic field

    if stronger: electromagnetic storms would be too severe.

    if weaker: inadequate protection from hard stellar radiation.

13. thickness of crust

    if thicker: too much oxygen would be transferred from the
    atmosphere to the crust.

    if thinner: volcanic and tectonic activity would be too great.

14. albedo (ratio of reflected light to total amount falling on surface)

    if greater: runaway ice age would develop.

    if less: runaway greenhouse effect would develop.

15. oxygen to nitrogen ratio in atmosphere

    if larger: advanced life functions would proceed too quickly.

    if smaller: advanced life functions would proceed too slowly.

16. carbon dioxide and water vapor levels in atmosphere

    if greater: runaway greenhouse effect would develop.

    if less: greenhouse effect would be insufficient.

17. ozone level in atmosphere

    if greater: surface temperatures would be too low.

    if less: surface temperatures would be too high; there would be
    too much uv radiation at the surface.

18. atmospheric electric discharge rate

    if greater: too much fire destruction would occur.

    if less: too little nitrogen would be fixed in the atmosphere.

19. oxygen quantity in atmosphere

    if greater: plants and hydrocarbons would burn up too easily.

    if less: advanced animals would have too little to breathe.

20. seismic activity

    if greater: too many life-forms would be destroyed.

    if less: nutrients on ocean floors (from river runoff) would not
    be recycled to the continents through tectonic uplift.

About a dozen more parameters, including several atmospheric characteristics, currently are being researched for their sensitivity in the support of life. However, the twenty listed in Table 12.1 in themselves lead safely to the conclusion that much fewer than a trillionth of a trillionth of a percent of all stars will have a planet capable of sustaining advanced life. Considering that the universe contains only about a trillion galaxies, each averaging a hundred billion stars,[g] we can see that not even one planet would be expected, by natural processes alone, to possess the necessary conditions to sustain life.[h] No wonder Robert Rood and James Trefil,[15] among others,[33] have surmised that intelligent physical life exists only on the earth. It seems abundantly clear that the earth, too, in addition to the universe, has experienced divine design.

Creator or chance?

In spite of all this evidence for design, some atheists claim that our existence is simply testimony to the fact that the extremely unlikely did, indeed, take place by chance. In other words, we would not be here to report the event unless that highly unlikely event actually took place. A reply to this argument has been developed by philosopher William Lane Craig:

> Suppose a dozen sharpshooters are sent to execute a prisoner by firing squad and the prisoner survives. The prisoner could conclude, since he is alive, that all the sharp-

---

g. The average number of planets per star is still uncertain. Research suggests that only bachelor stars similar to the sun may possess planets. Many young stellar objects appear to have accretion disks, but the heavy elements comprising such disks have only been available recently. Regardless, an extreme upper limit would be three planets per star.

h. The accepted assumption is that all life is based on carbon. Silicon and boron at one time were considered candidates for alternate life chemistries. However, silicon can sustain amino acid chains no more than about a hundred such molecules long. Boron may allow a little more complexity but has the disadvantage of being relatively scarce in the universe.

shooters missed by some extremely unlikely chance. He may wish to attribute his survival to an incredible bit of good luck, but he would be far more rational to conclude that the guns were loaded with blanks or that the sharpshooters all deliberately missed.

man, the Creator?

The growing evidence of design would seem to provide further convincing support for the belief that the God of the Bible, the God who lives beyond the limits of time and space, personally shaped the universe and Earth. Paul Davies concedes that "the impression of design is overwhelming."[34] A designer must exist. Yet, for whatever reasons, a few astrophysicists suggest that perhaps the designer is not God. But, if the designer is not God, who is? The alternative, some suggest, is man himself.

The evidence proffered for man as the creator comes from an analogy to delayed-choice experiments in quantum mechanics where it appears that the observer can influence the outcome of quantum mechanical events. With every quantum particle there is an associated wave. This wave represents the probability of finding the particle at a particular point in space. Before the particle is detected there is no specific knowledge of its location—only a probability of where it might be. But, once the particle has been detected, its exact location is known. In this sense, the act of observation is said by some to give reality to the particle. What is true for a quantum particle, they continue, may be true for the universe as a whole.

American physicist John Wheeler sees the universe as a gigantic feedback loop.

> The Universe [capitalized in his text] starts small at the big bang, grows in size, gives rise to life and observers and observing equipment. The observing equipment, in turn, through the elementary quantum processes that terminate on it, takes part in giving tangible "reality" to events that occurred long before there was any life anywhere.[35]

133

In other words, the universe creates man, but man through his observations of the universe brings the universe into reality. George Greenstein is more direct in positing that "the universe brought forth life in order to exist ... that the very cosmos does not exist unless observed."[36] Here we find a reflection of the question debated in freshmen philosophy classes across the land:

If a tree falls in the forest, and no one is there to see it or hear it, does it really fall?

Quantum mechanics merely shows us that in the micro world of particle physics man is limited in his ability to measure quantum effects. Since quantum entities at any moment have the potential or possibility of behaving either as particles or waves, it is impossible, for example, to accurately measure both the position and the momentum of a quantum entity (the Heisenberg uncertainty principle). By choosing to determine the position of the entity, the human observer has thereby lost information about its momentum.

It is not that the observer gives "reality" to the entity, but rather the observer chooses what aspect of the reality of the entity he wishes to discern. It is not that the Heisenberg uncertainty principle disproves the principle of causality, but simply that the causality is hidden from human investigation. The cause of the quantum effect is *not* lacking, *nor* is it mysteriously linked to the human observation of the effect after the fact.[i]

---

i. One can easily get the impression from the physics literature that the Copenhagen interpretation of quantum mechanics is the only accepted philosophical explanation of what is going on in the micro world. According to this school of thought, "1) There is no reality in the absence of observation; 2) Observation creates reality." In addition to the Copenhagen interpretation physicist Nick Herbert outlines and critiques six different philosophical models for interpreting quantum events.[37] Physicist and theologian Stanley Jaki outlines yet an eighth model.[38] While a clear philosophical understanding of quantum reality is not yet agreed upon, physicists do agree on the results one expects from quantum events.

This misapplication of Heisenberg's uncertainty principle is but one defect in but one version of the new "observer-as-creator" propositions derived from quantum physics. Some other rejoinders are presented here:

- Quantum mechanical limitations apply only to micro, not to macro, systems. The relative uncertainty approaches zero as the number of quantum particles in the system increases. Therefore, what is true for a quantum particle would not be true for the universe as a whole (assuming no coherent amplification).

- The time separation between a quantum event and its observed result is always a relatively short one (at least for the analogies under discussion). A multi-billion year time separation is far too long.

- The arrow of time has never been observed to reverse, nor do we see any traces of a reversal beyond the scope of our observations. Time and causality move inexorably forward. Therefore, to suggest that human activity today can affect events billions of years ago is nothing short of absurd.

- Intelligence, or personality, is not a factor in the observation of quantum mechanical events. Photographic plates, for example, are perfectly capable of performing observations.

- Both relativity and the gauge theory of quantum mechanics, now established beyond reasonable question by experimental evidence,[39] state that the correct description of nature is that in which the human observer is irrelevant.

Science has yet to produce a shred of evidence to support the notion that man created his universe.

the universe as God?

In *The Anthropic Cosmological Principle*, British astronomer John Barrow and American mathematical physicist Frank Tipler[40] begin by reviewing evidences for design of the universe, then go on to address several radical versions of the anthropic principle, including Wheeler's feed-back loop connection between mankind and the universe. Referring to such theories as PAP (participatory anthropic principle), they propose, instead, FAP (final anthropic principle).

In their FAP, the life that is now in the universe (and, according to PAP, created the universe) will continue to evolve until it reaches a state of totality that they call the Omega Point. At the Omega Point:

> Life will have gained control of all matter and forces not only in a single universe, but in all universes whose existence is logically possible; life will have spread into all spatial regions in all universes which could logically exist, and will have stored an infinite amount of information including all bits of knowledge which it is logically possible to know.[41]

In a footnote they declare that "the totality of life at the Omega Point is omnipotent, omnipresent, and omniscient!"[42] Let me translate: the universe created man, man created the universe, and together the universe and man in the end will become the Almighty God. Martin Gardner gives this evaluation of their idea:

> What should one make of this quartet of WAP, SAP, PAP, and FAP? In my not so humble opinion I think the last principle is best called CRAP, the Completely Ridiculous Anthropic Principle.[43]

In their persistent rejection of an eternal transcendent Creator, cosmologists seem to be resorting to more and more ludicrous alternatives. An exhortation from the Bible is appropriate: "See to it that no one takes you captive through hollow and deceptive philosophy."[44]

insufficient universe

It is clear that man is too limited to have created the universe. But, it is also evident that the universe is too limited to have created man. The observable universe contains no more than 10^{80} baryons[j] [k] and has been in existence for no more than 10^{18} seconds.

Compared to inorganic systems comprising the universe, biological systems are enormously complex. The genome (complete set of chromosomes necessary for reproduction) of an E. coli bacterium has the equivalent of about two million nucleotides. The human genome contains about six billion nucleotides. Moreover, unlike inorganic systems, the *sequence* in which the individual components are assembled is critical for the survival of biological systems.[l] Additional complications arise in the processes of protein synthesis common to all biological systems:

- Multiple special enzymes (themselves enormously complex sequence-critical molecules) are required to bind messenger RNA to ribosomes before protein synthesis can begin or end.

- Only amino acids with left handed configurations can be used in protein

- Each amino acid must be activated by a specific enzyme.

- Most mutations apparently are *not* spontaneous (i.e. random),[45, 46] yet certain adaptive "evolutionary" processes would require a multiplicity of spontaneous mutations.[47]

---

j. Baryons are protons and other fundamental particles, such as neutrons, that decay into protons.

k. For additional discussion about this limit for the universe, see footnote "m" in chapter 5.

l. A common rebuttal is that not all nucleotides and amino acids in organic molecules must be strictly sequenced. One can destroy or randomly replace about 1 nucleotide or amino acid out of 100 without doing damage to the function of the molecule. This is vital since life necessarily exists in a sequence-disrupting radiation environment. However, this is equivalent to writing a computer program that will tolerate the destruction of 1 statement of code out of 100! In other words, this error-handling ability of organic molecules constitutes a far more unlikely occurrence than strictly sequenced molecules.

- even the early earth (four billion years ago) had oxidizing conditions that would make the spontaneous chemical evolution of life virtually impossible.[48]

My point is that the universe is at least ten billion orders of magnitude ($10^{10,000,000,000}$ times) too small or too young for life to have assembled itself by natural processes.[m] Such calculations have been made by researchers, both theists and non-theists, in a variety of disciplines.[49-63]

Invoking other universes cannot solve the problem. All multi-universe models require that the additional universes remain totally out of contact with one another; that is, their space-time manifolds cannot overlap. Therefore, they cannot help resolve origin of life problems on Earth. The only explanation left for how living organisms received their complex and ordered configurations is that an intelligent, transcendent Creator personally infused this information.

Again we see that a personal, transcendent Creator must have brought the universe into existence.[n] A personal, transcendent Creator must have designed the universe. A personal, transcendent Creator must have designed planet Earth. A personal, transcendent Creator must have designed life.

---

m. Some may become skeptical about these conclusions when the remains of life are someday discovered on Mars. Such a discovery may be inevitable. However, it will not mean that spontaneous generation works. Rather, both the solar wind and ejected debris from asteroid collisions have the capacity to carry life materials from Earth to Mars.[64 - 66]

n. My use of the word *must* here is in the context of practical certainty, i.e. overwhelming likelihood, as opposed to absolute certainty. Human investigation can never yield absolute proof for anything, but it can yield practical proof.

PART THREE

Biblical Cosmology

As the controversies within scientific cosmology have been resolved, so have the supposed conflicts between science and the Bible. When both the facts of nature and the words of the Bible are responsibly interpreted, they yield a consistent revelation of God and His message to mankind.

CHAPTER THIRTEEN

Biblical Evidence for Long Creation Days

summary

Many scientists and others have regarded Christianity as an absurd belief system, or at best as a "religious," and by that they mean non-rational, faith. Why? Often it is because the book on which Christianity is based, the Bible, has been said to date the origin of the universe at 4004 B.C., or some such recent date. Seldom considered and discussed are the dozen or more different indicators from the Bible that a literal reading of Genesis demands an ancient, rather than a recent, creation date.

early biblical scholarship

Many of the early church fathers and other biblical scholars interpreted the creation days of Genesis 1 as long periods of time. The list includes the Jewish historian Josephus (1st century); Irenaeus, bishop of Lyons, apologist, and martyr (2nd century); Origen, who rebutted heathen attacks on Christian doctrine (3rd century); Basil (4th century); Augustine (5th century); and, later, Aquinas (13th century), to name a few.[1-5]

The significance of this list lies not only in the prominence of these individuals as biblical scholars, defenders of the faith, and pillars of the early church (except Josephus), but also in that their scriptural views cannot be said to have been shaped to accommodate secular opinion. Astronomical, paleontological, and geological evidences for the antiquity of the universe, of the earth, and of life did not come forth until the nineteenth century.

Ussher's chronology and fundamentalism

Archbishop Ussher's margin dates for the King James translation of the Bible (discussed in chapter 3) canonized in the minds of many English-speaking Protestants a creation date of 4004 B.C. for the universe and the earth. However, the accuracy or inaccuracy of this creation date did not become an issue for the Christian faith until the scientific developments of two centuries later. It moved into the spotlight as the fundamentalist movement began.

Fundamentalism got its start when two laymen, Milton and Lyman Stewart, sponsored the printing and distribution of twelve small books entitled *The Fundamentals: A Testimony of the Truth* (1909 - 1915). Organizationally, fundamentalism took shape when the World's Christian Fundamentals Association was formed at a conference in Philadelphia in 1919.

This association went farther than to require its members' adherence to the doctrine of creation and of the fall of man. It also identified evolution (i.e. Darwinism) as one of the great evils of our time, an enemy to be opposed from every angle and on every point. Because Ussher's short time scale was seen as the coup de grace to evolution, Ussher's chronology became incorporated into their "biblical" doctrine of creation.

Gosse's "appearance of age" theory

As scientific evidence mounted, Christians who were scientists began to recognize a dilemma. As early as the 1850's, British biologist and preacher Philip Gosse was forced to acknowledge that paleontological and physical data indicated an age for the earth far older than that permitted by Ussher's chronology, even if one conceded the possibility of some gaps in various genealogies. Gosse the scientist was convinced by the physical data, while Gosse the preacher was committed to what he thought was demanded by the Bible. What was he to do?

In 1857 Gosse published *Omphalos, an Attempt to Untie the Geological Knot.* In this book he maintained that God created the earth and life with the appearance of age—that the creation bore false records of a nonexistent past. He proposed, for example, that God made trees with annual rings for years that never existed.

The suggestion that God had written on the earth's rocks a superfluous lie hit a sour note with most of Gosse's fellow Christians. And, though his book stirred some interest at first, it soon fell into to disfavor.

Of late, however, Gosse's "appearance of age" idea has seen a revival. Gary North, a prominent "reconstructionist" theologian,[a] recently wrote:

> The Bible's account of the chronology of creation points to an illusion. ... The seeming age of the stars is an illusion. ... Either the constancy of the speed of light is an illusion, or the size of the universe is an illusion, or else the physical events that we hypothesize to explain the visible changes in light or radiation are false inferences.[6]

The Institute for Creation Research (ICR), a "scientific" proponent of Ussher's chronology, has held to the appearance of age since its inception in 1972.[7]

single revelational theology

Modern day advocates of Gosse's view typically hold what is called a single revelation view—the belief that the Bible is the only authoritative source of truth. In other words, we "must grope in darkness apart from God's

---

a. Reconstructionism, as taught by North and others, is a doctrinal system combining Puritan beliefs about law, politics, and biblical end-time events with Cornelius Van Til's theory (called "presuppositionalism") that all human reasoning and interpretation of scientific evidence must be subordinated to a "biblical" interpretation of reality. For a more thorough definition and a helpful analysis see *Dominion Debate: Kingdom Theology and Christian Restruction in Biblical Perspective* by Robert M. Bowman, Jr. (Grand Rapids: Baker Book House, 1991).

special revelation in scripture."[8] Accordingly, no tampering with the "literal" meaning of the Bible is tolerated. Henry M. Morris, ICR president, explains why:

> The road of compromise [on the issue of age], however attractive it seems, is a one-way street, ending in a precipice and then the awful void of "rational religion," or atheism. Our advice is to stay on the straight road of the pure Word of God.[9]

North agrees:

> For Christians to tamper with the plain meaning of the Bible in order to make it conform to the latest findings of this or that school of evolutionary thought is nothing short of disastrous.[10]

Those interpreting the Genesis creation days as six consecutive 24-hour periods have criticized those who posit long creation days for "interpreting the Bible through the glasses of science." They presume, of course, that deeply rooted scientific "assumptions" of an old universe provide the *only* basis for taking the Genesis creation days as long time periods.

secular response

One unfortunate result of the outspokenness of creationists holding to the young earth position is that most people now assume that *all* who believe God created the universe must subscribe to the young earth view and, worse yet, that the Bible directly states that the earth and all its life forms were created in six consecutive 24-hour days. Because of the implausibility of such a position, many reject the Bible out of hand without seriously investigating its message or even reading for themselves the relevant passages.

dual revelation theology

According to Psalm 19:1-4, the "words" of God proclaimed through the stars and galaxies have been heard by all people. In Romans 1:19-20, the Bible declares that everyone is "without excuse" as he or she faces God's eternal judgment [including those people who have never read the Bible or heard the preaching of believers] since what may be known about God has been made plain to *all* through what has been made. Colossians 1:23 points out that the plan of salvation "has been proclaimed to every creature under heaven." Table 13:1 provides a partial list of those Bible verses which indicate that God reveals Himself faithfully through the "voice" of nature as well as through the inspired words of scripture. Only this dual, and perfectly harmonious, revelation appears consistent with God's character and purpose.

For God to lie would be a violation of His holiness.[11] The Bible claims that God created the universe.[12] Further, it declares God responsible for the words of the Bible.[13] On this basis, no contradiction between the facts of nature and the facts of the Bible would be possible. Any apparent contradiction must stem from human misinterpretation.[b]

Table 13.1: Bible verses teaching that God reveals truth through His creation

Job 10:8-14	Psalm 50:6	Ecclesiastes 3:11
Job 12:7	Psalm 97:6	Habakkuk 3:3
Job 34:14-15	Psalm 98:2-3	Acts 17:24-31
Job 38 - 41	Psalm 104	Romans 1:18-25
Psalm 8	Psalm 139	Romans 2:14-15
Psalm 19:1-6	Proverbs 8:22-31	Colossians 1:23

---

b. Taken to its logical conclusion, the appearance of age theory would imply that we could not establish that our past existence actually occurred. For example, we could have been created just a few hours ago with the Creator implanting memory, material possessions, scars, and hardening of the arteries to make us appear and feel older than we really are. As such, we could not be held responsible for any of our "past" actions.

biblical basis for long creation days

The first chapter of Genesis declares that within six "days" God miraculously transformed a "formless and void" earth into a suitable habitat for mankind. The meaning of the word *day*, here, has become the center of a controversy. Does it, or does it not, make for a conflict between scripture and science?

The answer to that question depends upon whether the time periods indicated are 24 hours or, rather, something on the order of millions of years. Most Bible scholars (and scientists, too) would agree that a correct and literal interpretation of the creation "day" is one that takes into account definitions, context, grammar, and relevant passages from other parts of scripture. A careful analysis of all these elements yields many reasons for interpreting the creation days of Genesis as long periods of time. Here are some of them:

1. **Genesis 1 fits the form and, hence, the function of a biblical chronolog**. A study of all other chronologs in Scripture reveals that events presented in sequence are both time-order discernible and time-order significant. The significance is to show the orderly unfolding of God's plan and reveal His sovereign control, while the discernibility helps validate the message of His spokesmen. Key examples are found in Daniel 9:24-27 (a timetable for the rebuilding of Jerusalem, the Messiah's coming and death, the destruction of Jerusalem, years of desolation, restoration of temple sacrifices, the abomination, and then the end); Daniel 11:2-45 (a chronolog of the victories and defeats of various kings and kingdoms, including the final world ruler); and Revelation 8 - 9 (a sequential list of dooms preparatory to Christ's return to earth).

In the case of the creation days, long periods of time in which various life-forms were introduced in increasing abundance and complexity are, indeed, discernible and significant for validating the supernatural accuracy of the writer's statements. If all creation were completed in six

24-hour days, however, even the most sophisticated measuring techniques available would be totally incapable of discerning the sequence of events; and, thus, a major purpose of the chronolog would be thwarted.

2. **A long period of time is clearly acceptable with the definitions of *yowm*, *'ereb*, and *boqer*.** The Hebrew word *yowm*, translated *day*, may be used (and is) within the Bible, as it is in English, to indicate any of four time periods: a) from sunrise to sunset, b) from sunset to sunset, c) a segment of time without any reference to solar days (usually several years), and d) an age or epoch.

The Hebrew word *'ereb*, translated *evening* also means "sunset," "night," or "ending of the day." And the word *boqer*, translated *morning*, also means "sunrise," "coming of light," "beginning of day," or "dawning," with possible metaphoric usage (see Brown, Driver, and Briggs, *A Hebrew and English Lexicon of the Old Testament*, Oxford: Clarendon Press, 1980, also Harris, Archer, and Waltke, *Theological Wordbook of the Old Testament*, Chicago: Moody Press, 1980).

Some have argued for 24-hour days on the basis that *yowm*, when attached to an ordinal (second, third, fourth, etc.) elsewhere in the Bible always refers to a 24-hour period. This argument is inconclusive. The Bible, after all, has no other occasion to enumerate epochs of time. More importantly, no rule of Hebrew grammar states that *yowm* attached to an ordinal must refer to 24-hour days.

Others have argued that the Hebrew word *'olam* (as opposed to *yowm*) would have been used to indicate a long time period. However, Hebrew lexicons show that the word *'olam* only referred to a long age or period in postbiblical writings. In biblical times it meant "forever," "perpetual," "lasting," "always," "of olden times," or "the remote past, future, or both," but the range of its usage did not include a set period of time.[14, 15]

3. **The unusual syntax of the sentences enumerating specific creation days suggests indefinite time periods.** Looking at the word-for-word translation of the

Hebrew text, one finds this phraseology: "and was evening and was morning day Xth." The New International Version renders the time markers in this way: "And there was evening, and there was morning—the Xth day." The word arrangement, in both cases, is a departure from the simple and ordinary. It creates an ambiguity. If "day Xth" were intended as the noun complement for the one evening and morning together, the linking verb should appear just once, in plural form (as the King James Version renders it): "And the evening and the morning were the Xth day." We would expect the literal Hebrew to say, "and were evening and morning day Xth." But, that is not the case. This syntactic ambiguity does not constitute a proof. However, it does at least suggest an indefinite period for each phase of the creation.

4. **The seventh day in Genesis 1 and 2 is not closed out**. Of the first six creation days the Genesis writer says (New International Version): "...there was evening, and there was morning—the Xth day." This statement indicates that each of the first six creation days had a beginning and an ending. However, for the seventh creation day no such statement appears either in Genesis 1 - 2 or anywhere else in the Bible. Given the parallel structure for marking the creation days, this distinct change in form for the seventh day strongly suggests that this day has (or had) not yet ended.

Further information about the seventh day is given in Hebrews 4 and Psalm 95. Here we learn that God's day of rest continues even now. The writer of Hebrews says,

'On the seventh day God rested from all his work.' ... It still remains that some will enter that rest. ... There remains, then, a Sabbath-rest for the people of God; for anyone who enters God's rest also rests from his own work, just as God did from his. Let us, therefore, make every effort to enter that rest (Hebrews 4:4-10, NIV).

He indicates here that the seventh day of the creation week carries on through the centuries, from Adam and Eve, through Israel's development as a nation, through the time of Christ's earthly ministry, through the early days of the church, and on into future years. King David in Psalm 95:7-11 also refers to God's seventh day of rest as an ongoing event. From these passages we gather that the seventh day of Genesis 1 and 2 represents a minimum of several thousand years and a maximum that is open ended (though finite). It seems reasonable to conclude then, given the parallelism of the creation account, that the first six days also were very long time periods.

The fossil record provides another piece of evidence for an ongoing seventh day of rest. According to the fossils, more and more species of life came into existence through the millennia before modern man. Through time, the number of extinctions nearly balanced the number of introductions, but introductions remained slightly more numerous. Then came mankind. In the years of human history, the extinction rate has remained high while the introduction rate measures a virtual zero. Though estimates of the current extinction rate vary widely, from a low of one species per day to a high of five species per hour,[16, 17] and though man's influence upon that rate is significant,[18] even without man's impact at least one species per year goes extinct.[18, 19] At the same time, as biologists Paul and Anne Ehrlich report, "the production of a new animal species in nature has yet to be documented." Furthermore, "...in the vast majority of cases, the rate of change is so slow that it has not even been possible to detect an increase in the amount of differentiation."[20]

The creation days of Genesis, if long, provide an explanation. For six days God was introducing new life forms. After the creation of Adam and Eve, however, God ceased from His work of creating, and His rest, or "cessation," continues to this day.

5. **The events of the sixth day cover more than 24 hours.** Genesis 1 tells us that all the land mammals and *both* Adam and Eve were created on the sixth day. Genesis 2 provides further amplification, listing events between the creation of Adam and the creation of Eve. First, God

planted a garden in Eden, making "all kinds of trees to grow out of the ground." Then Adam worked and cared for the garden of Eden. After that, he carried out his assignment from God to name all the animals. In the process Adam discovered that none of these creatures was a suitable helper for him. Next, God put Adam into a deep sleep, performed an operation, awakened Adam, and introduced him to the newly created Eve. Adam's exclamation upon seeing Eve was *happa'am*. This expression is usually translated "now at length" (cf Genesis 29:34-35, 30:20, and 46:30 and Judges 15:3), roughly equivalent to our English expression, "At last." Finally, Adam and Eve received instructions from God concerning their responsibilities in managing the plants, animals, and resources of the earth. Many weeks', months', or even years' worth of activities took place in this latter portion of the sixth day.

Some 24-hour proponents argue that Adam's intelligence was so much higher before he sinned that he could do all these tasks at superhuman speed. This argument fails to account for Adam's response to Eve, and just as importantly, for the following points:

a) There is no biblical basis for suggesting that Adam functioned at superhuman speeds before he sinned.

b) Greater intellect would not significantly impact Adam's sixth-day tasks and experiences.

c) Adam in his perfect state would be all-the-more meticulous in performing his God-assigned tasks.

d) Jesus, though He was perfect in every way, did not perform His carpentry work and other everyday activities at a faster than normal rate.

6. **The wording of Genesis 2:4 suggests a long time span for the creation week.** This verse, a summary statement for the creation account, in the literal Hebrew reads, "These are the generations of the heavens and the earth when they were created in the day of their making ...." Here, the word *day* refers to all six creation days (and the creation events prior to the first creative day). Obviously, then, it refers to a period longer than 24

hours. Hebrew lexicons verify that the word for *generation* (*toledah*) refers to the time it takes a baby to become a parent or to a time period arbitrarily longer.[21] In Genesis 2:4 the plural form, *generations*, is used, indicating that multiple generations have passed.

7. **In describing the eternity of God's existence, Bible writers compare it to the longevity of the mountains or of the "foundations of the earth."** The figures of speech used in Psalm 90:2-6, Proverbs 8:22-31, Ecclesiastes 1:3-11, and Micah 6:2 depict for us the immeasurable antiquity of God's presence and plans. If these literary devices are used appropriately and accurately (as they must be, for they were inspired by God), then the earth and its foundations must reach back at least a few orders of magnitude beyond the relatively brief span of recorded history. Habakkuk 3:6 directly declares the mountains to be "ancient" and the hills to be "age-old," while II Peter 3:5 states that the heavens existed "long ago."

8. **Truthfulness and a purpose to reveal truth, both in the creation and the written Word, are fundamental attributes of God. He does not lie.** Numerous Bible verses explicitly declare that God is truthful, and that He does not mislead, either in word or in deed, those who seek to know the truth. Even that desire, itself, comes from Him. (See, for example, Psalm 119:160, Isaiah 45:19, Titus 1:2, Hebrews 6:18 and 11:6, and I John 5:6).

The implications are obvious. For God to create things with a deceptive "appearance" of age would violate His own stated character. Whatever objects of His creation we subject to theoretically valid and correctly applied (and interpreted) scientific analysis will reveal their true age.[c] We may assume that while God created

---

c. An inescapable conclusion of the "false age" theory, the idea that God made the universe appear old when, in fact, it is only about 10,000 years old, is that 99.9999999999999999% of the universe we observe is an illusion. For the radius of the universe that astronomers are convinced they study is about 10,000,000,000 light years, and the radius of that portion of the universe which, according to false-age proponents corresponds to things that have actually happened is only about 10,000 light years.

Adam and Eve with adult-sized bodies, He did not put into them twenty years' worth of deterioration. The abundant and consistent evidence, then, from astronomy, physics, geology, and paleontology for the age of the universe, the earth, and life must be taken seriously.

9. **The Bible affirms that the creation reveals God's existence, His handiwork, His power, and His divine nature.** Both Psalm 19 and Romans 1:20, among other passages, make clear that the physical universe we see is sufficient not only to prove that God really exists and that He created all things, but also to show mankind His qualities of love and power, provision and protection—to name just a few—so that "men are without excuse."

One must conclude, then, that honest scientific study leads to discovery of truths about God and His otherwise invisible qualities. This revelation of God via the universe implies that when God performs a miracle, He does not remove or distort the physical evidence of that miracle.[d]

10. **The Bible writers' statements about the vastness of the universe also serve as indicators of its age.** In Genesis 22:17, Jeremiah 33:22, and Hebrews 11:12, the number of God's children is compared with the number of stars in the sky and the number of grains of sand on the seashore—a "countless" number. For two reasons, this number must exceed a billion. First, since God's children include not only the Jews but also all those people who ever have or will trust in Him for salvation, that sum can be estimated conservatively to exceed two billion. Second, the Hebrew (and Greek) numbering systems included numbers up to the billions. Thus, "countless" would indicate a number at least one order of magnitude greater than billions, i.e. tens of billions. Given this number of stars as a minimum, and noting that

---

d. For example, spectral lines of stars and galaxies are broadened (by random motions of intervening matter) and the continuum red-shifted (by intervening dust) in direct proportion to the distance the light travels. Hence, the claim that God sent the star and galaxy light from points some 6000 light years distant (not from the objects) is invalid since the measured reddening and redshifting is consistent with light travel paths up to billions of light years long.

the stars are separated from each other by distances of about 4 light-years (not in a line, of course, but in a roughly spherical space), the diameter of the universe must exceed 20,000 light-years. And since no material in our universe moves more rapidly than the velocity of light (beyond the first 10^{-34} seconds), one can calculate that the age of the universe, then, must exceed 20,000 years.

According to recent findings, the number of stars in the universe totals approximately 10^{23} (a number that also approximates the sum of the grains of sand on the seashores). Again, using size to indicate age, 10^{23} stars separated from one another by about 4 light-years yield a minimum diameter of 200 million light years, thus a minimum age of 200 million years. (Note: Because God transcends space and time, He has the power to construct the universe at a rate more rapid than the velocity of light. But, the physical evidence shows that He did not do so.)

11. The sabbath day for man and sabbath year for the land are based on analogy with God's work week. God's fourth commandment says that the seventh day of each week is to be honored as holy, "for in six days the Lord made the heavens and the earth and rested on the seventh" (Exodus 20:10-11). As Hebrew scholar Gleason Archer asserts, "By no means does this demonstrate that 24-hour intervals were involved in the first six 'days,' any more than the 8-day celebration of the Feast of Tabernacles proves that the wilderness wanderings under Moses occupied only eight days."[22] Sometimes the sabbath is a full year (cf Leviticus 25:4), not a day. Clearly, the emphasis in Exodus 20 is on the principle of one out of seven, not on the duration of the days of creation.

12. The onset of "death through sin" does not restrict the length of creation days. Romans 5:12 says, "Sin entered the world through one man, and death through sin, and in this way death came to all men, because all sinned." Some interpret this as implying that no death of any kind occurred before the sin of Adam, and, hence, only a few days could possibly have transpired from the creation of the first life-forms to the sin of Adam. However, the absence of physical death would pose just as much a problem for three 24-hour days as it would for three billion years. Many species of life cannot survive even three hours without food, and the mere ingestion of food requires at least the death of plants or plant parts.

Recognizing the problems of reading Romans 5:12 as a statement about physical death, others have interpreted the verse as meaning "soulish" death. In the Genesis creation account, distinctions are made among merely physical animals (invertebrates and lower vertebrates), soulish animals (birds and mammals), and spirit creatures (human beings). The difficulty with this adjusted view is that soulish animals are not condemned to "death through sin." Of all life on Earth, only man earned the title "sinner."

The key point is that Romans 5:12 is addressing neither physical nor soulish death.[e] When Adam sinned, he instantly "died," just as God said he would ("In the day that you eat of it, you shall surely die"—Genesis 2:17). Yet, he remained alive physically and soulishly. He died spiritually. He lost his fellowship with God and gained a natural inclination to defy God. Genesis 3 records that after Adam died (spiritually) through sin, God sent an angel to block Adam's access to the tree of life.

13. The subjection of the creation to "its bondage of decay" does not restrict the length of creation days. Romans 8:20-21 says, "For the creation was subjected to frustration, not by its own choice, but by the will of the one who subjected it, in hope that the creation itself will be liberated from its bondage to decay and brought into the glorious freedom of the children of God." Some claim this passage implies that Adam's sin ushered in physical death, natural decay, and increasing entropy. They conclude that decay and death did not occur until Adam sinned. Thus, the time from the universe's creation to Adam's fall must be brief enough to explain the lack of evidence for a period devoid of decay and death.

---

e. In addition to "death through sin," the book of Romans addresses several different kinds of death.

While it is obvious that freedom from decay could not extend through billions of years, it is less obvious but equally certain that it could not last for even one 24-hour day. Without decay, work (at least in the current universe) would be impossible. Without work, physical life would be impossible. But, life did exist, according to Genesis 1, at least from the third creation day onward. Thus, Romans 8:20-21 could not be inferring that Adam's sin inaugurated the process of decay.

It is just as likely that the text refers to another kind of decay, the disorder in man's life that resulted from his rebellion against God. In Genesis 1:28 God commanded man to maintain his environment. But, since man first sinned, the opposite has occurred. Man's effect upon his environment is analogous to the results of sending a two-year-old to tidy up a closet. As one would need to wait for the two-year-old to grow up a little before expecting him to properly tidy up a closet, so, too, the creation (and the replacement of this universe with a new one) must wait for the human race to overcome its problem of sin.

bogus evidences for a young universe

For the reasons addressed by North and Morris, "scientific creationists" who hold to a 24-hour creation day insist that evidences for an old universe and Earth are inconclusive and that there is, by contrast, considerable evidence supporting a young age. Here they are sadly misguided and are misguiding many whose science education and biblical training are inadequate to aid them in evaluation. All of these "evidences" of youthfulness, involve one or more of the following problems:

- faulty assumptions
- faulty data
- misapplication of principles, laws, and equations
- ignorance of mitigating evidence

Ironically, these fallacious arguments, when corrected, provide some of the strongest evidences available for an old universe and an old earth. Examples appear below:

Argument A: The continents erode too quickly.

Measurements show that the continents are lowered by wind, rain, etc. at a rate of 0.05 millimeters per year. At this rate, the continents—averaging about 800 meters in elevation—would disappear in about 16 million years. Since continents do still have considerable elevation, the earth must be younger than 16 million years.

Reply: The fallacy of Argument A lies in failing to recognize that lava flows, continental shelf buildup (from eroded material), coral reef buildup, and uplift from colliding tectonic plates occur at rates roughly equivalent to, and in a few cases far exceeding, the erosion rate. The Himalayas, for example, rise at about 15 millimeters per year.

Argument B: The earth's magnetic field decays too rapidly.

The strength of the earth's magnetic field has been decreasing steadily since measurements were first taken some 150 years ago. Based on the field strength of a typical magnetic star (certainly exceeding any conceivable value for the earth) and on the observed rate of decay, some creationists have calculated that the decay process must have begun no more than 10,000 years ago. Thus, the earth's age must be 10,000 years or less.

Reply: The oversight in Argument B is that the earth's magnetic field does not undergo steady decay but rather follows a "sinusoidal" pattern. That is, the field decays, builds up, decays, builds up, etc. The proof for this pattern lies in ancient geologic strata found throughout the world. The rocks reveal that the earth's field reverses its polarity about every half million years—the reversal process itself lasting roughly 10,000 years.[23]

Argument C: The sun burns by gravitational contraction and is, therefore, relatively young.

Before the discovery of nuclear energy the only explanation astronomers could offer for the enormous energy output of the sun and other stars was gravitational contraction. Given the diameter and energy output of our sun, we can calculate that its maximum age would be 100 million years—*if* it were expending energy only by this process. When some measurements indicated a slight decrease in the sun's diameter, a number of creationists were quick to conclude that the sun's energy source must indeed be gravity, rather than nuclear fusion; and, thus, the sun's age must be less than 100 million years.

Reply: Again, the argument overlooks significant data. First, it has been shown that if a body of our sun's size were experiencing gravitational contraction, the temperature and pressure at its center would be such as to ignite nuclear fusion. Furthermore, the measured characteristics of the sun, including its effective temperature, luminosity, spectra, radius, and mass, all indicate that the sun certainly is burning by nuclear fusion and that this fusion has been proceeding for about 5 billion years.

As for the observed decrease in the sun's diameter, the measurements cited were later found to conflict other visual measurements. The conflict has since been laid to rest completely by the much more precise work of Barry LaBonte and Robert Howard.[24] Their measurements, within a limit of 0.1 arc seconds, show no change in the solar radius over the years from 1974 to 1981.

Argument D: The galaxy clusters are not dispersed.

In order for a cluster of heavenly bodies to remain together, the gravity of the system must be able to rein in the velocities of the individual bodies within it. Armed with measurements of velocities and masses, astronomers can calculate (a) the dispersal time for clusters whose total mass is too small for gravitational containment, and (b) the relaxation time (the time required for the bodies to assume randomized velocities) for clusters whose total mass is large enough for containment. Some creationists point out that when such calculations are applied to galaxy clusters, the lack of galaxy dispersal indicates an age for the clusters much less than a billion years.

Reply: The problem with Argument D is that these calculations not only assume that we are seeing all the mass within the galaxy clusters but also assumes that the galaxies are point sources. On the contrary, there is sound evidence for concluding that most of the mass is not seen (see chapter 10). Also, galaxies are not good point sources. In fact, their diameters are only about one order of magnitude smaller than the average distances between them, within a given cluster. Therefore, these dispersal-time calculations are virtually meaningless.

By comparison, virtually all of the mass within star clusters is visible, and star cluster stars *are* point sources. The average distances between them are at least seven orders of magnitude greater than their average diameters. When dispersal and relaxation time calculations are applied to star clusters in our galaxy, many clusters show their ages to be greater than two billion years.

Other arguments for instantaneous creation, i.e. for a young universe and earth, can similarly be exposed as fallacious. They are omitted only to save space.

age of the universe

There are hundreds of legitimate and reliable scientific tools for demonstrating that the creation (except modern man) is much older than Archbishop Ussher's chronology states. In just the last several years the age of the universe itself, and hence a date for the events of Genesis 1:1, has been open to direct astronomical measurement. Several methods now exist for determining the date of the creation of the universe. The results of the application of these methods appear in Table 13.2 and reveal a level of consistency that permits the secure conclusion[f] that the universe is roughly 16 billion years old.

---

f. A description of the security of this conclusion comes from California Institute of Technology's physicist and Nobel Laureate Murray Gell-Mann. In his comments to the supreme court (about the balanced treatment act) he said that it would be easier to believe that the world is flat, not round, than to believe the universe is only 6000 years old, not about 15 billion.

Table 13.2: Measurements of the age of the universe

measuring method	age (billions of years)
expansion of the universe	14.5 ± 5.0
color-luminosity fitting	17.0 ± 2.4
nucleochronology	17.0 ± 4.0
anthropic principles	17 ± 7

mean age = 16 ± 3 billion years

advent of modern man

According to Genesis 1, the origin of the universe predates the six days of creation, while the origin of man occurs at the very end of the six days. Thus, the creation of the universe would predate by far the creation of man. Biblical genealogies serve as an indicator of how recently man appeared. However, they provide a loose measure only. The problem lies in the usage of the Hebrew words for father and son, *'ab* and *ben*. *'Ab* can just as well refer to the grandfather, great-grandfather, great-great-grandfather, etc. Similarly, *ben* could be a grandson, great-grandson, etc. In the book of Daniel, Belshazzar's mother refers to Nebuchadnezzar as her son's father when, in fact, two other kings separate them, and they are not even related. Such flexibility in the usage of *'ab* and *ben* explains why parallel genealogies (e.g. I Chronicles 3, Matthew 1, and Luke 3) are often at variance with one another. The best Hebrew scholarship places the biblical date for the creation of Adam between 10,000 and 35,000 years ago (the outside limits being 6,000 and 50,000 years).

In Genesis 1, God speaks of *adham* (male and female), and only *adham*, as being made in His image. The point is emphasized by repetition. Clearly, as man's story unfolds through subsequent chapters, one discovers that what makes him different is a quality called "spirit." Man is unique among all species of life. By "spirit" the Bible means "aware of God and capable of forming a relationship with Him." Evidence of man's spiritual dimension would include divine worship, shown by religious relics, altars, and temples. From the Bible's perspective, decorating, burial of dead, or use of tools would not qualify as conclusive evidence of the spirit. Moreover, non-spirit creatures such as bower birds decorate their nests, elephants bury their dead, and chimpanzees use tools.

While bipedal, tool-using, large-brained hominids roamed the earth at least as long ago as one million years,[25 - 27] evidence for religious relics and altars dates back only 8,000 to 24,000 years.[28, 29] Thus, the secular anthropological date for the first spirit creatures is in complete agreement with the biblical date.

Some differences, however, between the Bible and secular anthropology remain. The Bible not only would deny that the hominids were men, it also would deny that Adam was physically descended from these hominids. Even here, support from anthropology is emerging. New evidence indicates that the hominid species may have gone extinct before, or as a result of, the appearance of modern man.[30, 31] At the very least, "abrupt transitions between [hominid] species" is widely acknowledged.[32, 33]

divine craftsmanship

One further consideration from an altogether different perspective concerns the nature of creativity itself. Observe any skilled sculptor, painter, or poet, a craftsman of any kind. Observe the painstaking yet joyful labor poured into each object of his design. Examine the creation on any scale, from a massive galaxy to the interior of an atom, from a whale to an amoeba. The splendor of each item, its beauty of form as well as of function, speaks not of instantaneous mass production, but rather of time and attention to detail, of infinite care and delight. Such delight is expressed throughout Genesis 1 in the oft-repeated statement, "And God saw that it was good."

CHAPTER FOURTEEN

Genesis Creation Account

summary

The "higher critics" of the last two centuries have badly misinterpreted the first two chapters of Genesis, and by their error led many astray. Establishing the correct point of view and initial conditions for the Genesis creation chronologies yields a sequence of events in perfect harmony with modern science. This accuracy is too amazing for Moses to have guessed. He must have received divine help.

Among nineteenth century leaders of seminaries and churches, reaction to Kant's cosmology and its scientific support took two distinct directions. One camp, led by German theologians, made concessions and adjustments in their view of the scriptures. The other camp, championed by British and American fundamentalists, stood utterly opposed, denigrating science and reason and upholding the scriptures.

higher criticism theology

A cloud over biblical veracity had arisen even before the publication of Kant's works. The first scholars to publish serious claims for multiple authorship and internal inconsistencies in the Genesis account of creation were Richard Simon, an Oratorian priest, writing in 1678,[1] and Campegius Vitringa, a Dutch Reformed theologian, writing in 1707.[2] Their works, though, were largely ignored by their contemporaries and forgotten by later generations.

In 1753 a French physician, Jean Astruc, perhaps out of a desire to justify his immorality,[3] published a treatise undermining the credibility of Genesis. He concluded that in writing Genesis, Moses (or someone later) had interwoven material from several independent sources. In particular, he said that Genesis 1 and 2 contained two contradictory creation narratives of different authorship.[4-6]

Not long after Astruc's ideas began circulating, Johann Eichhorn, the most famous theologian of his day, published the same conclusions as Astruc.[a, 7] He further pointed out that the discoveries of geologists not only contradicted both Genesis chronologies but also the creation date proposed by Ussher. Soon Eichhorn and his German colleagues were theorizing that much of the Old Testament was a compilation of late, unreliable documents dating from 800 to 500 B.C. They saw the biblical accounts of creation as edited versions of borrowed myths.

The methodology of Astruc, Eichhorn, and the emerging "higher critics" was notably "simplistic." They presumed that the order of mention for the creation events represented the intended chronology of the text. Verb tense, indicators of parenthetical comment, and other syntactic features were ignored. The order of Genesis creation events they deduced appears in Table 14.1.[8, 9]

As a result of their view of the chronologies, many theologians concluded that the Bible was unreliable, not only internally, but also with respect to science and history. Therefore, for them, God became discoverable only through another channel, through "faith" alone. Their brand of faith, then, was totally subjective. It comprised moral responses prompted by the conscience and warm feelings about the presence of God. Thus, their position, theologically and scientifically, was hardly distinguishable from Kant's.

---

a. Though Eichhorn does not cite Astruc, he admits his dependence in *Einleitung in das Alte Testament* [Introduction to the Old Testament], *2nd edition.* (Leipzig: 1787), pp. 246-247.

Table 14.1: Genesis creation events according to higher critics

Genesis 1 order of events	Genesis 2 order of events
1. heavens and earth created	1. heavens and earth created
2. light created	2. plant life created
3. light divided from darkness	3. man (male only) created
4. heaven ("firmament") created	4. animal life created
5. land separated from water	5. woman made from man's side
6. plant life created	
7. Sun, Moon, and stars created	
8. animal life created	
9. man (male and female) created	

fundamentalist reaction

Many who held the Bible to be totally error free reacted to Kant's conclusions and to the new discoveries in astronomy and geology with flat rejection. They denied the possibility that any physical phenomena had taken more than a few thousand years to occur. All forms of evolution,[b] whether astronomical, geological, or biological, were rejected outright. All scientific discoveries were subordinated to the inviolable dogma of Archbishop Ussher's chronology.

In seeing through the interpretative errors of the higher critics' chronology for Genesis 2, they removed the internal contradictions. But, unwittingly, they failed to question the faulty interpretation of Genesis 1.[10] Thus they trapped themselves, unawares, into denying not only the scientific timescales, but even the best established

---

b. Strictly speaking, evolution refers to change over a period of time, long or short. The change may be gradual or punctuated, developmental or detrimental, natural or supernatural.

principles of physics and astronomy. Their view required, for example, that the earth, light, and water predate the formation of the sun and the stars.[c]

Their position, then, necessitated a denial of God's revelation of truth via nature and an acceptance of the written word, the Bible, as the *only* reliable revelation of truth. Ironically, their definition of faith resembled that of their opponents, the higher critics. In both cases faith in God lost its factual footing, it was removed from the reach of testing by scientific and historical data.

the scientific method

What Astruc, Eichhorn, and the higher critics failed to do, among other things, was to recognize the scientific method in the text. Interestingly, the scientific method, to a large extent, originated from renaissance experimenters' perception of certain consistent patterns in Scripture. In describing sequences of physical events, the Bible always begins with a statement of the point of view, or frame of reference. Next, there is an indication of the initial conditions. Then comes a chronological account of the physical events. Finally, there is the conclusion of the matter. Here, in a nutshell, is the scientific method.

integrating Genesis 1 and 2

Without question, the description of creation in Genesis 1 is markedly different from that in Genesis 2. However, an examination of the point of view in each passage clarifies why. Genesis 1 focuses on the physical events of creation; Genesis 2, on the spiritual events. More specifically, Genesis 1 describes those miracles God performed to prepare the earth for mankind. Genesis 2 presents God's assignment of authority and responsibility.

---

c. This means that the earth must not only form by itself, but that liquid water must exist and plants must survive for a time at temperatures of 454 degrees F below zero (-270°C)!

Careful attention to verb tenses and to the purpose of each account eliminates any supposed contradiction between Genesis 1 and 2. Plants, rain, man, animals, and woman are subjects of discussion in Genesis 2, but creation chronology is not the issue. The man (Adam) simply interacts first with the plants, then with the animals, and last of all, with the woman (Eve). His role with respect to each is delineated.[d]

origin of the universe

The Bible opens with this declaration: "In the beginning God created the heavens and the earth." The Hebrew words for heavens and earth are *shamayin* and *erets*. Whenever these two words are joined together in Hebrew literature they refer to the entire physical universe.[15, 16] The Hebrew word for "created," *bara*, refers always to divine activity. The word emphasizes the newness of the created object. It means to bring something entirely new, something previously non-existent, into existence.[17] Genesis 1:1 speaks of God's creating—originating—the fundamental constituents (all the space, time, matter, energy, galaxies, stars, planets, etc.) of the universe.

specific point of view

Unfortunately, most Bible commentaries still err with Jean Astruc and the higher critics in placing the point of view for Genesis 1 out in the heavens, looking down on

---

d. The Hebrew language has only three verb tenses: imperative, perfect, and imperfect. The perfect tense denotes completed actions while the imperfect tense denotes incomplete or unfinished actions. The use of the perfect tense in Genesis 2:19 for the formation of the beasts and the birds simply implies that those creatures were made sometime in the past. Nothing in the verb tenses or the context of Genesis 2 would necessitate the existence of man before the beasts and the birds or, for that matter, the trees of the garden of Eden.[11 - 14]

the earth. Yet, the second verse of Genesis 1 places the point of view *under* the cloud cover, on the surface of the waters (see Figure 14.1). It says, "The Spirit of God was hovering over[e] the surface of the waters." This one seemingly minute correction eliminates any supposed contradiction between the biblical order of events and the scientific order. The miracles described in the account take place in or under the earth's atmosphere, not in the broader scope of outer space.

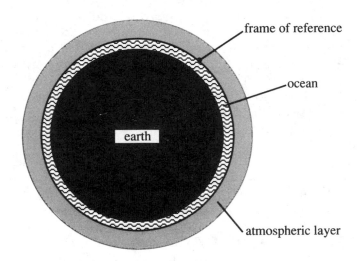

Figure 14.1: The frame of reference for Genesis 1

The point of view from which the creation events are described is the surface of the ocean, below the cloud layer, as stated in verse 2.

---

e. The Hebrew verb here, *rachaph*, actually connotes "brooding" or "vivifying." Hence, this statement may imply biblical support for formation of the first life-forms in the oceans.[18]

initial conditions

Genesis 1:2 also states for us three initial conditions of planet earth:

- It was dark upon the surface of the ocean.
- The earth was formless, or disorganized.
- The earth was void or empty.

Since Genesis 1 focuses on the introduction of life upon the earth, formless and void (or disorganized and empty) are best interpreted in the context of life. That is, the Bible says that in its initial state, the earth was unfit to support life and was literally "empty" of life. We are told, too, that the earth's atmosphere (and/or interplanetary debris) blocked out the light that exists throughout the universe. Light could not pass through to the surface.

The physics of star and planet formation verifies that the proto-earth indeed must have had an atmosphere (or debris cloud) opaque to light. Such studies also confirm that conditions of the proto-earth made it entirely unfit for the support of life.

order of creation events

With the point of view and initial conditions established, we can properly interpret the biblical chronolog of events. What once seemed baffling or incorrect now becomes comprehensible and demonstrably accurate. It may be helpful to note, too, that six different Hebrew verbs are used for God's creative work. Table 14.2 lists the eleven major milestones in order, giving suitable English equivalents for those verbs. *Bara* appears in the manuscripts only twice more after Genesis 1:1, once for the creation of *nephesh*, or soulish animals—those creatures endowed with mind, will, and emotions (namely, birds and mammals)—and again for the creation of *adam*, or "spirit" beings—those creatures endowed with the capacity to respond to God Himself.

Table 14.2: Order of Genesis 1 creation events[f]

1. creation of the physical universe (space, time, matter, energy, galaxies, stars, planets, etc)

2. transformation of the earth's atmosphere from opaque to translucent

3. formation of a stable water cycle

4. establishment of continent(s) and ocean(s)

5. production of plants on the continent(s)

6. transformation of the atmosphere from translucent to transparent (Sun, Moon, and stars became visible for the first time)

7. production of small sea animals

8. creation of sea mammals (*nephesh*)

9. creation of birds [possibly same time as 8] (more *nephesh*)

10. making of land mammals (wild mammals, mammals that can be domesticated, and rodents—still more *nephesh*)

11. creation of mankind (*adam*)

no coincidence

The record given in Table 14.2 perfectly accords with the findings of modern science. Ironically, some have found fault with it for its simplicity and brevity. We must remember, first, that the recorder of the events, Moses, lived some 3500 years ago, and he was writing not only for the people of his time and culture but for all people of all times and cultures. Use of the simplest possible terms was essential. Second, the apparent purpose of the account is to document various demonstrations of God's miraculous power in forming the earth and life upon it. With obvious necessity, the account is selective. Only the highlights, those events most important for achieving God's final goals, are included. As a result, dinosaurs, for example, receive no particular mention.

f. For a more detailed discussion of these creation events, see *Genesis One: A Scientific Perspective*.[19]

The odds that Moses could have guessed the correct order even if he were given the events are 1 chance in 11x10x9x8x7x6x5x4x3x2x1, or 1 chance in roughly 40 million. In addition, Moses scored three for three in describing the initial conditions. Of course, most amazing of all is the accuracy of his depiction of each creative event. Clearly, Moses must have been inspired by God to write as he did.

CHAPTER FIFTEEN

The Problem of Suffering and Evil

summary

To many cosmologists, including Einstein, Hoyle, and Davies, the existence of suffering, evil, and death seems incompatible with a reality of an all-powerful, all-loving Creator. These "scourges," they say, make sense only if an impersonal force or intelligence initiated the universe and established the mechanisms for biological evolution. The point they have missed is that God's plan, according to the Bible, is to develop eternally perfect people without disturbing free-will. This plan can only be achieved by the operation of God's perfect mercy and justice through pain, suffering, and death, and, most significantly, through the temptations offered by the most powerful created being.

typical reaction to creation evidence

While many prominent cosmologists have been pushed by compelling physical evidence to concede the necessity of a Creator for the universe, few have embraced the Creator-God of the Bible. The list of rejectors includes such luminaries as Albert Einstein, Fred Hoyle, Paul Davies, and George Greenstein. Their stumbling block is an issue of concern not only to cosmologists but to people from all backgrounds and walks of life, including theologians. It is the question, "How can we explain evil and suffering?"

The explanation proffered by these famed scientists and many others is simple: God is impersonal[a] and, therefore, uncaring. The evil, suffering, and death are merely a consequence of evolutionary processes, in particular, of survival of the fittest, that the creator set in motion.

the failure of clerics

Albert Einstein, for one, posed the question of evil and suffering to many rabbis and priests during most of his life without ever receiving a satisfactory answer. Typically, these religious leaders responded by saying that God has not revealed the answer to us yet. They encouraged patient endurance and blind trust in the All-knowing One.

Regrettably, Einstein and many others lacked the patience and persistence to pursue an answer further. They took for granted the biblical knowledge of these religious professionals and assumed that the scriptures failed to address this crucially important issue. Of what value, then, could such a "revelation" be?

biblical solution to the problem

How sad that in all their studies, so many clerics could have missed the answer. It is not a simple one, of course. In fact, it is sufficiently involved to warrant book-length treatment. Neither is it possible, in this brief space, to address the deep emotional impact that suffering and evil makes upon an individual life. What I present here is merely an outline of key points in the biblical solution to the problem:

a. This suggested impersonality for God contradicts the established facts of nature. The transcendence of the creation event, the established design characteristics of the universe, the earth, and life, and the harmony, beauty, and elegance of the laws of nature all imply that the Creator must be a personal being.

1. **People are not robots.**

   Man was sinless when God created him (Genesis 2-3).

   If God had forceably prevented man from sinning, man's will would not be free.

   Without free choice, real love is impossible.

2. **God's ultimate plan is to perfect those who choose to be perfected.**

   In the new creation man will retain his free will, but there will be no sin, no suffering, no death, no evil (Revelation 21:4).

   Only (and all) those who overcome sin and evil by choosing to worship Christ, rather than to live for self, can enter into this perfect state (Revelation 21:7-8).

   The perfecting process takes place via the interaction of our will and Christ's in opposition to Satan's will (Acts 8:23, Philippians 2:13, II Thessalonians 3:5, II Timothy 2:26).

3. **All people now sin. All enter life in a state of spiritual incapacitation.**

   Through Adam's trespass, sin has been imputed to each human (Romans 5:12-21).

   We are sinners, by nature, from conception (Psalm 51:5).

   Without God's restraint and influence we would be totally depraved (Jeremiah 17:9, John 16:8-11).

   On our own, nothing we do is righteous by God's standard (Isaiah 64:6, John 15:5, Romans 3:10-20).

4. **What is spiritual is eternal.**

   All spiritual beings are created to exist forever. They cannot be annihilated (Daniel 12:2, Matthew 25:46).

   Man's conscience confirms that his existence continues after physical death (Ecclesiastes 3:11).

   Spiritual death refers to man's incapacity to do good and, unless he entrusts himself to the goodness of Christ, results in his eternal separation from God (Romans 5:12-21).

5. **Life on Earth has an eternal purpose.**

This life is roughly analogous to a school course with a final examination.

This life is intended to prepare us for the eternity that lies ahead (I Corinthians 6:2-3, I Peter 2:9).

Only one chance and only so much time is needed for an individual to choose (or reject) God's offer and to choose (or reject) God's training (Luke 16:19-31, Hebrews 9:27).

Neither too much nor too little time would be good for us (Isaiah 38-39, Isaiah 57:1-2, Acts 5:1-10).

6. **Physical death has a good purpose.**

God gave us physical death so that we might have the possibility of being rescued from spiritual death (Genesis 3:22-24).

Death seals and protects the righteousness of the one who chooses God (I Kings 14:12-13, Isaiah 57:1-2).

Death limits the degradation and punishment of the one who rejects God (Romans 1:32).

Death limits the spread of wickedness in society (Genesis 19).

7. **Suffering has a purpose.**

Suffering alerts us to potentially destructive problems—physical, emotional, and spiritual (II Corinthians 7:8-13).

Suffering restrains us, keeping us from committing evil (Hebrews 12:5-13).

Suffering humbles us, reminding us of our weakness (II Corinthians 12:7-10).

Suffering teaches us about ourselves, our values, our choices (Matthew 13:20-23).

Suffering teaches us about God—the magnitude of His love for us in His willingness to suffer and die in our place (Hebrews 12:2).

8. **God is involved in our suffering.**

God identifies personally with the sufferings of human beings (Matthew 25:31-46).

God personally has suffered and has been tempted more than anyone (Isaiah 50:4-7, Isaiah 52:13 - 53:12).

God is at work through His Spirit to restrain evil, to call people to repent of their evil and to submit to His authority over their lives (John 16:8-11, Joel 2:32, John 14:15-23).

God promises that all things will work together for good for those who love Him and are called to His purpose (Romans 8:28).

9. **Man's short lifespan and suffering bring spiritual protection.**

Long life-spans promote the wicked, not the righteous (Genesis 6:3-8).

Absence of suffering promotes the wicked, not the righteous (Genesis 3:16-19).

10. **Innocence is available in Christ alone.**

Man's conscience speaks to him of a God whose standard is perfection—perfection in love, perfection in obedience to His moral code, obedience in action, word, and thought (I Samuel 6:20, Isaiah 59:2-14, Habakkuk 1:12-13).

Only a perfect being can meet that standard (Deuteronomy 32:4, I Samuel 2:2).

Through His life, death, and bodily resurrection, Jesus Christ proved Himself to be the perfect one, the one and only redeemer of sinful man (Hebrews 2:9-15).

11. **Human solutions fail to solve our problem.**

Even with the best possible government, worldwide peace and justice, unparalleled prosperity, unprecedented good health, and lifespans in the hundreds of years, most people, when the chance arises, will choose rebellion and evil (Revelation 20:1-10).

Minimizing the consequences of sin fails to check its spread (Genesis 4:11-13, Hebrews 12:5-13).

Punishment for sin is necessary for restraint and correction, but it is insufficient to eliminate sin.

Only God has the power to conquer Satan, sin, and death (Isaiah 43:10-11 & 59:15-16).

12. It is good that Satan initiated evil and is the tempter.

Because Satan is the most powerful created being, and because the circumstances in which he is tempting us are the most severe, there exists no possibility of our facing any greater test than the one we undergo in our brief physical life on earth (Isaiah 14:11-17, Ezekiel 28:12-19, Jude 9).

If we pass this test, choosing God's rescue in Christ, the way is opened for God to deliver us eternally from all sin, death, suffering, and evil *without* taking away our free-will, and without losing the possibility to love.

In order for our rescue to be eternally secure, everyone must be subjected to the ultimate test (Rev. 20:7-10).

13. The test is not too difficult.

God will not allow us to be tempted beyond what we are able to bear (I Corinthians 10:13).

God's help and comfort are always available to those who depend upon Him (Matthew 28:20, Hebrews 13:5).

14. Suffering that aligns with God's will shows the power of the gospel.

Those who exchange their guilt for Christ's innocence gain, through the trials in their lives, perseverance, maturity, and God's perfect joy (James 1:2-4).

Suffering within God's will purifies the soul and communicates to the world the surpassing value of the spiritual over the physical, the eternal over the temporal (Hebrews 12:16, I Peter 2:19-25 & 4:1-2) .

Skeptics watch Christians' response to suffering and persecution to see whether or not the faith of such people is true, reliable, and secure, to see whether or not God is miraculously at work within them (I Peter 3:13-18).

The severest, often unacknowledged, test to which doubters subject believers is persecution (Job, Acts 7:55-8:3 & 9:1-19).

One of the greatest joys of this life comes through suffering for "righteousness' sake" (Matthew 5:10, I Peter 4:14).

15. Our time of suffering is brief.

Our lifespan is like a whiff of smoke compared to eternity (Job 7:6-10, Psalm 103:15-16, James 4:14).

We can barely begin to fathom God's time frame (II Timothy 1:9, 1:2, II Peter 3:8, Revelation 21:1).

16. God has a purpose in blessing the wicked.

God always reaches to us first through His mercy and grace and then through His justice and rebukes (John 3:16-18, II Peter 3:9).

God first blesses those going astray so that they may acknowledge Him as the source of their blessing and then repent (Psalm 73).

If people refuse to acknowledge God as the source of their blessing, God removes the blessing and thus prepares them to listen to the message of those who have chosen Him (Proverbs 24:15-20).

If the wicked persist in wickedness, they receive only what they have chosen—eternal torment and separation from God (Psalm 73).

17. Both heaven and hell are expressions of God's perfect love.

Nobody dies without having the clear, understood opportunity to receive or reject God's offer of forgiveness for sin and of life with Him (John 3:16-21).

Just as it is impossible, from a human perspective, to imagine how awful the torment in hell could be and how anyone could possibly deserve the punishment, it is equally impossible to imagine how wonderful heaven could be and how anyone could possibly deserve the blessing (I Corinthians 2:9).

Those who go to hell are those who prefer eternal torment to obedience to God and fellowship with Him (Luke 12:8-10, Hebrews 6:4-6, Hebrews 10:26-29).

Scripture tells of differing degrees of torment in hell—the greater the wickedness, the greater it will be (Rev. 20:11-15)—and of differing rewards in heaven, depending on one's degree of submission to the work of God's Spirit in building Christlikeness (I Corinthians 3:12-15).

If God imposed no torment in hell, the residents there would vex one another to an unthinkable degree (Jeremiah 17:9). One purpose of the torment is to restrain the expression of evil. Some need more restraint than others.

why so long?

Another common question asks why God takes so long to resolve the problem of evil and suffering. From the perspective of the Creator, however, the problem is resolved quickly. If the time since the creation of the universe were scaled down to a single year, the whole of human history would be less than one minute.

CHAPTER SIXTEEN

The Gospel According to the Creation

summary

The Bible is the only religious text that teaches a cosmology in full agreement with the latest astrophysical discoveries. The plan of salvation as stated in the Bible can be seen through observation of the universe around us. Thus, all human beings have a chance to discover it. The Bible is the only one of all religious writings which declares a message in full agreement with (and, of course, amplification of) the gospel message seen in creation.

biblical cosmology

The preceding chapters document how the latest discoveries on the frontiers of astronomy and physics validate (and expand upon) biblical cosmology. Table 16.1 reviews some examples of that cosmology. Moreover, the Bible among all "holy books" stands uniquely apart in its statements about cosmology. No other "sacred" writings teach an extra-dimensional reality independent of the dimensions of our universe. Most, in fact, flatly contradict it.

Table 16.1: Some biblical statements of cosmological significance

1. God existed before the universe. God exists totally apart from the universe, and yet can be everywhere within it. (Genesis 1:1, Colossians 1:16-17)

2. Time (for the universe) has a beginning. God's existence and activity precede this created time. (II Timothy 1:9, Titus 1:2)

3. The Son of God, Jesus Christ created the universe. He has no beginning and was not created. (John 1:3, Colossians 1:16-17)

4. God created the universe from that which cannot be detected with the five human senses. (Hebrews 11:3)

5. After His resurrection Jesus could pass through walls in His physical body, an evidence of His extra-dimensionality. (Luke 24:36-43, John 20:26-28)

6. Jesus, operating in His extra-dimensionality, can do far more for us than would ever be possible if He was confined to the dimensions of the universe. (John 14:12 & 16:5-7, Phil. 2:5-11)

7. God is very near, yet we cannot see Him, a further evidence of His extra-dimensionality. (Exodus 33:20, Deuteronomy 30:11-14, John 6:46)

8. God designed the universe in such a way that it would support human beings. (Genesis 1 & 2, Nehemiah 9:6, Job 38, Psalm 8:3, Isaiah 45:18)

creation gospel

"Since the creation of the world, God's invisible qualities—his eternal power and divine nature—have been clearly seen, being understood from what has been made, so that man is without excuse." "This is the gospel that you heard and that has been proclaimed to every creature under heaven." These words from Romans 1:19-20 and Colossians 1:23 clarify that, according to the Bible, everyone has the opportunity to know God. His/her response to the evidences in the creation is a key factor. As the previous chapters briefly review, the evidence is awesome both in quantity and quality—especially to our generation.

More than speaking merely of God's existence, the creation, according to Romans 1, also reveals essential truths about God's character, which would include His desire and means to form a relationship with man. As an illustration of the accessibility of that information, the Bible includes an account of an ancient character, Job (Job 7 - 19), who *without* the aid of scriptures, and in opposition to the religion of his peers, discerned all the elements of "the gospel," the good news of how man can find eternal life in God. Here is a review of those elements:

A Creator must exist. Living things do not make themselves. No organism ever has been observed to spontaneously assemble itself.

The Creator must have awesome power and wisdom. The quantity of material and the power resources within our universe are mind-boggling. The information, or intricacy, manifest in any part of the universe, and especially in a living organism, is beyond our ability to comprehend. And what we see is only what God has shown us within our dimensions of space and time!

The Creator must be loving. The simplicity, balance, order, elegance, and beauty seen throughout the whole of the creation demonstrates that God is loving rather than capricious. Further, the capacity and desire to nurture, and to protect, seen in so many creatures, only make sense if their Creator possesses these same attributes. It is apparent that God cares for all of His creatures, for He has provided for their needs.

The Creator must be just and must require justice. Inward reflection and outward investigation affirm that human beings have a conscience. When conscience is violated, guilt is incurred and shame is felt. The conscience reflects the reality of right and wrong and the necessity of obedience.

Each of us falls hopelessly short of the Creator's standard. We incur guilt when we violate any part of God's moral law in our actions, our words, and our thoughts. Who can keep his thoughts and attitudes perfectly pure for even an hour? If each person falls hopelessly short of his or her own standards, how much more so of God's?

Because the Creator is loving, wise, and powerful, He must have made a way to rescue us. When we come to despair over our helpless imperfection, we can begin to understand from the creation around us that God's love, wisdom, and power are sufficient to deliver us from our otherwise hopeless situation.

If we trust our lives totally to the Rescuer, we will be saved. The one and only path is to give up all human attempts to satisfy God's requirements and to put our trust solely in Him and in His means of redemption.

The creation, thus, reveals all the necessary steps to develop a right relationship with God. These steps are uniquely corroborated by the Bible. All other "sacred" writings preach a different message. Moreover, the Bible reveals the specific means of God's rescue—God's one and only Son, sent to earth to live a sinless life, to die on our behalf, taking upon Himself the full penalty for our offenses against God, and to rise from the dead so that in trusting Him for forgiveness and in giving Him full authority over our lives we will be granted eternal life.

extra-dimensional Christian living

As vital as the new cosmology may be for convincing the skeptic that Jesus Christ is his one and only LORD and Savior, it is also important as an aid to Christians in living day to day. Christians are transformed and strengthened as they become convinced, truly convinced, that the

Savior they cannot see is every bit as real and close as the person closest to them—even closer. Further, all the paradoxical doctrines in the Bible[b] (e.g. the Trinity, free-will and predestination, eternal security, baptism in the Holy Spirit, heaven, hell, spiritual gifts) can be resolved and understood within the context of extra-dimensional reality.[c] Again, the implications and possibilities of extra-dimensionality, not only for living the Christian life but also for resolving the age-old controversies within Christendom, would make for one or several book-length works.

---

b. The existence of paradoxical doctrines in the Bible that cannot be resolved without appeal to extra-dimensional reality constitutes evidence that the Bible's message came from an extra-dimensional source. The fact that such paradoxical doctrines are missing from the holy books of the other religions suggests that these books simply stem from human origin.

c. The extra dimensions discussed in this book constitute a minimum realm of operation for the Creator. He may function in many more dimensions. He may even operate in dimensions completely independent from space and/or time.

CHAPTER SEVENTEEN

Conclusion of the Matter

A review of developments in the study of our universe and its origin reveals a pattern: As atheistic and agnostic researchers have been repeatedly and progressively pointed by the evidence toward a personal Creator, they have devised more and more bizarre loopholes to escape these findings. This misguided ingenuity will doubtless continue until the return of Christ. However, the evidence for a universe designed, initiated, shaped, and sustained exactly as the Bible describes, by God, continues to mount.

Certainly, Kantian philosophy has been overthrown, and we would do well to identify its vestiges in modern society and reshape our thinking accordingly. Though much more remains to be researched and discussed about cosmology and its theological implications, the only rational response to the mountain of evidence accumulated thus far is to surrender one's life to the God of the Bible.

References

ONE: **The Odd Couple**

1. Eddington, Arthur S. "The End of the World: from the Standpoint of Mathematical Physics," in *Nature 127.* (1931), p. 450.
2. Hoyle, Fred. "A new Model for the Expanding Universe," in *Monthly Notices of the Royal Astronomical Society 108.* (1948), p. 372.
3. Davies, Paul. *God and the New Physics.* (New York: Touchstone, Simon and Schuster, 1983), p. viii.
4. Bavinck, Herman. *The Philosophy of Revelation.* (New York: Longmans, Green, 1909), p. 88.
5. Whitcomb, John C. and DeYoung, Donald B. *The Moon: Its Creation, Form, and Significance.* (Winona Lake, Indiana: BMH Books, 1978), p. 69.
6. *Ibid.,* p. 65.
7. Akridge, Russell. "A Recent Creation Interpretation of the Big Bang and Expanding Universe," in *Bible-Science Newsletter.* (May 1982), pp. 1, 4.
8. Ruse, Michael. *Darwinism Defended: A Guide to the Evolution Controversies.* (Reading, Massachusetts: Addison-Wesley, 1982), pp. 303, 321.

TWO: **Early Historical Roots**

1. Zimmer, Heinrich Robert. *Myths and Symbols in Indian Art and Civilization.* (Washington, D.C.: Bollingen Foundation, 1946), pp. 3-22.
2. Gombrich, R. F. "Ancient Indian Cosmology," in *Ancient Cosmologies.* edited by Carmen Blacker and Michael Loewe. (London: George Allen and Unwin, 1975), pp. 120-123.

3. Hamilton, Edith. *Mythology.* (New York: Mentor, 1969), p. 312.

4. Franz, Marie-Louise. *Patterns of Creativity Mirrored in Creation Myths.* (Zurich: Spring, 1972).

5. Oswalt, Wendell M. *Alaskan Eskimos.* (New York: Chandler, 1967), pp. 212-214.

6. Kilzhaber, Albert R. *Myths, Fables, and Folktales.* (New York: Holt, 1974), pp. 113-114.

7. Abell, George. *Exploration of the Universe.* (New York: Holt, Rinehart, and Winston, 1964), pp. 16-19.

8. Clagett, Marshall. *Greek Science in Antiquity.* (New York: Collier Books, 1955), pp. 116-118.

9. Fischer, Irene. "Another Look at Eratosthenes' and Posidonius' Determinations of the Earth's Circumference," in *Quarterly Journal of the Royal Astronomical Society, 16.* (1975), pp. 152-167.

10. Plato. "Republic: VII," 530, b and c, in *The Collected Dialogues of Plato.* edited by Edith Hamilton and Huntington Cairns. (New York: Bollingen Foundation, Pantheon Books, 1961), p. 762.

11. Schaff, Philip. *History of the Christian Church, volume V, The Middle Ages.* (Grand Rapids, Michigan: Wm. B. Eerdmans, 1907), p. 652.

12. Lucretius Carus, T. "The Nature of the Universe," in *Theories of the Universe,* edited by Milton K. Munitz. (Glencoe, Illinois: Free Press, 1957), p. 43.

13. North, J. D. *The Measure of the Universe: A History of Modern Cosmology.* (Oxford: Clarendon Press, 1965), p. 423.

14. Lucretius Carus, T. pp. 41-57.

15. Welch, C. A., Arnon, D. I., Cochran, H., Erk, F. C., Fishleder, J., Mayer, W. V., Pius, M., Shaver, J., and Smith, F. W. *Biological Science: Molecules to Man, blue version, revised edition.* (Boston: Houghton Mifflin, 1968). This has been the standard text in biology for many American public high schools.

16. Augustine. "The City of God," Book XVI, Chapter 9 in *Great Books of the Western World, volume 18, Augustine.* edited by Robert Maynard Hutchins. (Chicago: Encyclopædia Britannica, 1952), p. 428.

17. Gilson, Etienne. *History of Christian Philosophy in the Middle Ages.* (New York: Random House, 1955), pp. 229-231, 650-651.

18. Glenn, Paul J. *A Tour of the Summa.* (St. Louis, Missouri: B. Herder Book, 1960), p. 5.

19. Aquinas, Thomas. "The Summa Theologica," in *Great Books of the Western World, volume 19, Thomas Aquinas: I.* edited by Robert Maynard Hutchins. (Chicago: Encyclopædia Britannica, 1952), pp. 12-14.

THREE: **Rebirth of Science**

1. Thiel, Rudolph. *And There Was Light: The Discovery of the Universe.* (New York: Alfred A. Knopf, 1957), p. 73.
2. Abell, George. *Exploration of the Universe.* (New York: Holt, Rinehart, and Winston, 1964), pp. 43-45.
3. Hansen, James. "The Crime of Galileo," in *Science 81.* (March 1981), pp. 14-19.
4. Broderick, James. *Galileo: The Man, his Work, his Misfortunes.* (New York: Harper & Row, 1964), p. 76.
5. Newton, Isaac. "To the Reverend Dr. Richard Bentley, at the Bishop of Worcester's House, in Park Street, Westminster from Cambridge, December 10, 1692," in *Theories of the Universe.* by Milton K. Munitz. (Glencoe, Illinois: Free Press, 1957), pp. 211-212.
6. Johnson, Paul. *A History of Christianity.* (New York: Atheneum, 1976), p. 413.
7. Corben, H. C. and Stehle, Philip. *Classical Mechanics, 2nd edition.* (New York: John Wiley and Sons, 1960), pp. 77-83.
8. Chandrasekhar, S. *Principles of Stellar Dynamics.* (New York: Dover, 1960), pp. 193-209.
9. Mihalas, Dimitri and Routly, Paul McRae. *Galactic Astronomy.* (San Francisco: W. H. Freeman, 1968), pp. 172-176, 232-240.
10. Schwarzschild, Martin. *Structure and Evolution of the Stars.* (New York: Dover, 1965), pp. 30-120. This is a classic text stating the essential physics of star growth in an easy to follow manner.
11. Cox, John P. and Giuli, R. Thomas. *Principles of Stellar Structure, Volume 1: Physical Principles and Volume 2: Applications to Stars.* (New York: Gordon and Breach, 1968). This standard text reviews the subject of stellar aging in some detail.

FOUR: **Rise of Non-Theism**

1. Bruno, Giordano. "On the Infinite Universe and Worlds," in *Giordano Bruno, His Life and Thought with Annotated Translation of His Work, On the Infinite Universe and Worlds.* by Dorothea Waley Singer. (New York: Henry Schuman,1950), pp. 250-259.
2. Johnson, Francis R. "Thomas Digges and the Infinity of the Universe," in *Theories of the Universe.* edited by Milton K. Munitz. (Glencoe, Illinois: Free Press, 1957), pp. 184-189.

3. Swedenborg, Emanuel. *Principia Rerum Naturalium*. (Dresden, 1734).

4. Wright, Thomas. "An Original Theory of the Universe," in *Theories of the Universe*. edited by Milton K. Munitz. (Glencoe, Illinois: Free Press, 1957), pp. 225-230.

5. Thiel, Rudolf. *And There Was Light: The Discovery of the Universe*. (New York: Alfred A. Knopf, 1957), p. 218.

6. Randall, John Herman, Jr. *The Career of Philosophy, volume II*. (New York: Columbia University Press, 1965), p. 113.

7. Kant, Immanuel. "Universal Natural History and Theory of the Heavens," in *Theories of the Universe*. edited by Milton K. Munitz. (Glencoe, Illinois: Free Press, 1957), pp. 242-247.

8. Kepler, Johannes. "The Harmonies of the World," in *Great Books of the Western World, volume 16, Ptolemy, Copernicus, Kepler*. edited by Robert Maynard Hutchins. (Chicago: Encyclopædia Britannica, 1952), pp. 1005-1085.

9. Newton, Isaac. "Mathematical Principles of Natural Philosophy, Book III, General Scholium," in *Great Books of the Western World, volume 34, Newton, Huygens*. edited by Robert Maynard Hutchins. (Chicago: Encyclopædia Britannica, 1952), pp. 369-372.

10. Bromiley, Geoffrey W. *Historical Theology: An Introduction*. (Grand Rapids, Michigan: William B. Eerdmans, 1978), pp. 343-356.

11. Kant, Immanuel. "Critique of Pure Reason," in *Great Books of the Western World, volume 42, Kant*. edited by Robert Maynard Hutchins. (Chicago: Encyclopædia Britannica, 1952), p. 160.

12. Kant, Immanuel. *Religion Within the Limits of Pure Reason Alone*. translated by T. M. Green and H. H. Hudson. (New York: Harper and Row, 1960), pp. 131-133.

13. *Ibid.*, p. 182.

14. Kant, Immanuel. "Critique of Pure Reason," in *Great Books of the Western World, volume 42, Kant*. edited by Robert Maynard Hutchins. (Chicago: Encyclopædia Britannica, 1952), pp. 135-137.

15. *Ibid.*, pp. 160-161.

16. Bruno, Giordano. pp. 252-254.

17. Kant, Immanuel. "Universal Natural History and Theory of the Heavens," in *Theories of the Universe*. edited by Milton K. Munitz. (Glencoe, Illinois: Free Press, 1957), p. 240.

18. Schücking, E. L. "Cosmology," in *Relativity Theory and Astrophysics 1. Relativity and Cosmology* edited by Jurgen Ehlers. (Providence, Rhode Island: American Mathematical Society, 1967), p. 218.

19. Whipple, Fred L. *Earth, Moon, and Planets, revised edition*. (Cambridge, Massachusetts: Harvard University Press, 1963), pp. 34-36.

References

20. Grosser, Morton. *The Discovery of Neptune*. (Cambridge, Massachusetts: Harvard University Press, 1962), pp. 39-123.

21. Harrison, E. R. "The dark night-sky riddle: a 'paradox' that resisted solution," in *Science, 226*. (1984), pp. 941-945.

22. Jaki, Stanley L. *The Paradox of Olbers' Paradox*. (New York: Herder and Herder, 1969), pp. 72-143.

23. Trumpler, Robert J. "Absorption of Light in the Galactic System," in *Publications of the Astronomical Society of the Pacific, 42*. (1930), pp. 214-227.

FIVE: Scientists Rediscover God

1. Bondi, Herman. *Cosmology, second edition*. (Cambridge, United Kingdom: Cambridge University Press, 1960), p.21.

2. North, J. D. *The Measure of the Universe: A History of Modern Cosmology*. (Oxford: Clarendon Press, 1965), pp. 16-18.

3. Eisberg, Robert M. *Fundamentals of Modern Physics*. (New York: John Wiley and Sons, 1961), pp. 7-9.

4. Eisberg, Robert M., p. 14.

5. Abell, George. *Exploration of the Universe*. (New York: Holt, Rinehart, and Winston, 1964), pp. 99-101.

6. Einstein, Albert. "Zur Elektrodynamik bewegter Körper," in *Annalen der Physik, 17*. (1905), pp. 891-921. The English translation is in *The Principle of Relativity* by H. A. Lorentz, A. Einstein, H. Minkowski, and H. Weyl with notes by A. Sommerfeld and translated by W. Perrett and G. B. Jeffrey (London: Methuen and Co., 1923), pp. 35-65.

7. Einstein, Albert. "Ist die Trägheit eines Körpers von seinem Energieinhalt abhängig?" in *Annalen der Physik, 18*. (1905), pp. 639-644. The English translation is in *The Principle of Relativity* by H. A. Lorentz, A. Einstein, H. Minkowski, and H. Weyl with notes by A. Sommerfeld and translated by W. Perrett and G. Jeffrey (London: Methuen and Co., 1923), pp. 67-71.

8. Eisberg, Robert Martin. *Modern Physics*. (New York: John Wiley and Sons, 1961, pp. 30-35.

9. *Ibid.*, pp. 37-38, 75-76, 580-592.

10. Jackson, John D. *Classical Electrodynamics*. (New York: John Wiley and Sons, 1962), pp. 352-369.

11. Lamoreaux, S. K., Jacobs, J. P., Heckel, B. R., Raab, F. J., and Forston, E. N. "New Limits on Spatial Anisotropy from Optically Pumped ^{201}Hg and ^{199}Hg," in *Physical Review Letters, 57,* (1986), pp. 3125-3128.

12. Einstein, Albert. "Die Feldgleichungen der Gravitation," in *Sitzungsberichte der Königlich Preussischen Akademie der Wissenschaften.* (1915), Nov. 25, pp. 844-847. (The following reference includes this reference.)

13. Einstein, Albert. "Die Grundlage der allgemeinen Relativitätstheorie," in *Annalen der Physik, 49.* (1916), pp. 769-822. The English translation is in *The Principle of Relativity* by H. A. Lorentz, A. Einstein, H. Minkowski, and H. Weyl with notes by A. Sommerfeld and translated by W. Perrett and G. B. Jeffrey (London: Methuen and Co., 1923), pp. 109-164.

14. Einstein, Albert. "Erklärung der Perihelbewegung des Merkur aus der allgemeinen Relativitätstheorie," in *Sitzungsberichte der Königlich Preussischen Akademie der Wissenschaften.* (1915), Nov. 18, pp. 831-839.

15. Dyson, F. W., Eddington, A. S., and Davidson, C. "A Determination of the Deflection of Light by the Sun's Gravitational Field, from Observations made at the Total Eclipse of May 29, 1919," in *Philosophical Transactions of the Royal Society of London, Series A, 220.* (1920), pp. 291-333.

16. Weinberg, Steven. *Gravitation and Cosmology: Principles and Applications of the General Theory of Relativity.* (New York: John Wiley and Sons, 1972), p. 198.

17. Van Biesbroeck, G. "The Relativity Shift at the 1952 February 25 Eclipse of the Sun," in *Astronomical Journal, 58.* (1953), pp. 87-88.

18. Counselman III, C. C., Kent, S. M., Knight, C. A., Shapiro, I. I., Clark, T. A., Hinteregger, H. F., Rogers, A. E. E., and Whitney, A. R. "Solar Gravitational Deflection of Radio Waves Measured by Very-Long-Baseline Interferometry," in *Physical Review Letters, 33.* (1974), pp. 1621-1623.

19. Shapiro, I. I., Pettengill, G. H., Ash, M. E., Ingalls, R. P., Campbell, D. B., and Dyce, R. B. "Mercury's Perihelion Advance: Determination by Radar," in *Physical Review Letters, 28.* (1972), pp. 1594-1597.

20. Taylor, J. H., Fowler, L. A., and McCulloch, P. M. "Measurements of General Relativistic Effects in the Binary Pulsar PSR 1913+16," in *Nature, 277.* (1979), pp. 437-440.

21. Taylor, J. H. "Gravitational Radiation and the Binary Pulsar," in *Proceedings of the Second Marcel Grossmann Meeting on General Relativity, Part A.* edited by Remo Ruffini. (Amsterdam: North-Holland Publishing, 1982), pp. 15-19.

22. Shapiro, Irwin I., Counselman III, Charles C., and King, Robert W. "Verification of the Principle of Equivalence for Massive Bodies," in *Physical Review Letters, 36.* (1976), pp. 555-558.

References

23. Pound, R. V. and Snider, J. L. "Effect of Gravity on Nuclear Resonance," in *Physical Review Letters, 13.* (1964), pp. 539-540.

24. Reasenberg, R. D., Shapiro, I. I., MacNeil, P. E., Goldstein, R. B., Breidenthal, J. C., Brenkle, J. P., Cain, D. L., Kaufman, T. M., Komarek, T. A., and Zygielbaum, A. I. "Viking Relativity Experiment: Verification of Signal Retardation by Solar Gravity," in *Astrophysical Journal Letters, 234.* (1979), pp. 219-221.

25. Vessot, R. F. C., Levine, M. W., Mattison, E. M., Blomberg, E. L., Hoffman, T. E., Nystrom, G. U., and Farrel, B. F. "Test of Relativistic Gravitation with a Space-Borne Hydrogen Maser," in *Physical Review Letters, 45.* (1980), pp. 2081-2084.

26. Porcas, R. W., Booth, R. S., Browne, I. W. A., Walsh, D., and Wilkinson, P. N. "VLBI Observations of the Double QSO 0957+561 A, B," in *Nature, 282.* (1979), pp. 384-386.

27. Weymann, R. J., Latham, D., Angel, J. R. P., Green, R. F., Liebert, J. W., Turnshek, D. A., Turnshek, D. E., and Tyson, J. A. "The Triple QSO PG 1115+08: Another Probable Gravitational Lens," in *Nature, 285.* (1980), pp. 641-643.

28. Henry, J. Patrick and Heasley, J. N. "High-Resolution Imaging from Mauna Kea: the Triple Quasar in 0.3 arc s Seeing," in *Nature, 321.* (1986), pp. 139-142.

29. Langston, G. I., Conner, S. R., Lehar, J., Burke, B. F., and Weiler, K. W. "Galaxy Mass Deduced from the Structure of Einstein Ring MG1654+1346," in *Nature, 344.* (1990), pp. 43-45.

30. Slusher, Harold S. *The Origin of the Universe: An Examination of the Big Bang and Steady State Cosmogonies, revised edition.* (El Cajon, California: Institute for Creation Research, 1980).

31. Barnes, Thomas G. II. *Physics of the Future: A Classical Unification of Physics.* (El Cajon, California: Institute for Creation Research, 1983).

32. Slusher, Harold S. and Ramirez, Francisco. *The Motion of Mercury's Perihelion: A Reevaluation of the Problem and Its Implications for Cosmology and Cosmogony.* (El Cajon, California: Institute for Creation Research, 1984).

33. Akridge, Russell. "A Recent Creation Interpretation of the Big Bang and the Expanding Universe," in *Bible-Science Newsletter, May 1982.* pp. 1-4 and *June 1982.* p. 7.

34. Craig, William Lane. *The Kalam Cosmological Argument.* (London, U. K.: Macmillan Press, 1979), pp. 63-153.

SIX: **The Expanding Universe**

1. Einstein, Albert. "Kosmologische Betrachtungen zur allgemeinen Relativitätstheorie," in *Sitzungsberichte der Königlich Preussischen Akademie der Wissenschaften.* (1917), Feb. 8, p. 142-152. The English translation is in *The Principle of Relativity* by H. A. Lorentz, A. Einstein, H. Minkowski, and H. Weyl with notes by A. Sommerfeld and translated by W. Perrett and G. B. Jeffrey (London: Methuen and Co., 1923), pp. 175-188.

2. Einstein, Albert. "Die Feldgleichungen der Gravitation," in *Sitzungsberichte der Königlich Preussischen Akademie der Wissenschaften.* (1915), Nov. 25, pp. 844-847 (included in the following reference).

3. Einstein, Albert. "Die Grundlage der allgemeinen Relativitätstheorie," in *Annalen der Physik, 49.* (1916), pp. 769-822. English translation is in *The Principle of Relativity* by H. A. Lorentz, A. Einstein, H. Minkowski, and H. Weyl; notes by A. Sommerfeld; and translated by W. Perrett and G. B. Jeffrey (London: Methuen, 1923), pp. 109-164.

4. Eddington, Arthur S. "On the Instability of Einstein's Spherical World," in *Monthly Notices of the Royal Astronomical Society, 90.* (1930), p. 668.

5. *Ibid.,* pp. 668-678.

6. North, J. D. *The Measure of the Universe: A History of Modern Cosmology.* (Oxford, U. K.: Clarendon Press, 1965), pp. 125-129.

7. Petrosian, Vahé. "Confrontation of Lemaître Models and the Cosmological Constant with Observations," in *Proceedings of the I. A. U. Symposium No. 63: Confrontation of Cosmological Theories with Observational Data,* edited by M. S. Longair. (Dordrecht-Holland, Boston-U.S.A., D. Reidel Publishing, 1974), pp. 38-39.

8. Brecher, Kenneth and Silk, Joseph. "Lemaître Universe, Galaxy Formation and Observations," in *Astrophysical Journal, 158.* (1969), pp. 91-102.

9. de Sitter, Willem. "On Einstein's Theory of Gravitation, and its Astronomical Consequences, Third Paper" in *Monthly Notices of the Royal Astronomical Society, 78.* (1917), pp. 3-28.

10. Robertson, H. P. "On Relativistic Cosmology," in *Philosophical Magazine and Journal of Science, 5, seventh series.* (1928), pp. 835-848.

11. Friedmann, Alexandre. "Über die Krümmung des Raumes," in *Zeitschrift Für Physik, 10.* (1922), pp. 377-386.

12. Friedmann, Alexandre. "Über die Möglichkeit einer Welt mit konstanter negativer Krümmung des Raumes," in *Zeitschrift Für Physik, 21.* (1924), pp. 326-332.

13. Hubble, Edwin. "A Relation Between Distance and Radial Velocity Among Extra-Galactic Nebulae," in *Proceedings of the National Academy of Sciences, 15.* (1929), pp. 168-173.

References

14. Jastrow, Robert. *God and the Astronomers.* (New York: W. W. Norton, 1978), pp. 27-28.

15. Eddington, Arthur S. "On the Instability of Einstein's Spherical World," in *Monthly Notices of the Royal Astronomical Society, 90.* (1930), pp. 668-678.

16. Eddington, Arthur S. "The End of the World: from the Standpoint of Mathematical Physics," in *Nature, 127.* (1931), pp. 447-454, in particular p. 450.

17. Omer Jr., Guy C. "A Nonhomogeneous Cosmological Model," in *Astrophysical Journal, 109.* (1949), pp. 164-176.

18. Einstein, Albert. "Spielen Gravitationsfelder in Aufbau der materiellen Elementarteilchen eine wesentliche Rolle," in *Sitzungberichte der Königlich Preussischen Akademie der Wissenschaften.* (1919), April 10, pp. 349-356.

19. Douglas, A. Vibert, "Forty Minutes With Einstein," in *Journal of the Royal Astronomical Society of Canada, 50.* (1956), p. 100.

20. Barnett, Lincoln. *The Universe and Dr. Einstein.* (New York: William Sloane Associates, 1948), p. 106.

21. Einstein, Albert. *Out of My Later Years.* (New York: Philosophical Library, 1950), pp. 27-28.

22. *Ibid.,* pp. 26-30.

23. *Ibid.,* p. 27.

SEVEN: Cosmic Hesitation

1. Hubble, Edwin. "A Relation Between Distance and Radial Velocity Among Extra-Galactic Nebulae," in *Proceedings of the National Academy of Sciences, 15.* (1929), p. 173.

2. Hubble, Edwin and Humason, Milton L. "The Velocity-Distance Relation Among Extra-Galactic Nebulae," in *Astrophysical Journal, 74.* (1931), pp. 43-80.

3. Lemaître, Georges. *Annales de la Société scientifique de Bruxelles, Tome XLVII, série A, première partie.* (April, 1927), p.49. The English translation of this paper is given in the following reference.

4. Lemaître, Georges. "A Homogeneous Universe of Constant Mass and Increasing Radius accounting for the Radial Velocity of Extra-Galactic Nebulae," in *Monthly Notices of the Royal Astronomical Society, 91.* (1931), pp. 483-490.

5. Lemaître, Georges. "The Expanding Universe," in *Monthly Notices of the Royal Astronomical Society, 91.* (1931), pp.490-501.

6. Lemaître, Georges. reply to Sir James Jeans in *Nature, 128.* (1931), p. 704.

7. Eddington, Arthur S. "On the Instability of Einstein's Spherical World," in *Monthly Notices of the Royal Astronomical Society, 90.* (1930), pp. 668-678.

8. *Ibid.*, p. 672.

9. Eddington, Arthur S. "The End of the World: from the Standpoint of Mathematical Physics," in *Nature, 127.* (1931), p. 450.

10. Lemaître, Georges. "The Beginning of the World from the Point of View of Quantum Theory," in *Nature, 127.* (1931), p. 706.

11. Lemaître, Georges. *The Primeval Atom: An Essay on Cosmogony,* translated by Betty H. and Serge A. Korff. (New York: D. Van Nostrand, 1950), pp. 99-100.

12. Lemaître, Georges. Reply to Sir James Jeans in *Nature, 128.* (1931), p. 706.

EIGHT: Steady State Cosmology

1. North, J. D. *The Measure of the Universe.* (Oxford, U. K.: Clarendon Press, 1965), pp. 125-129, 223-228.

2. MacMillan, William Duncan. "On Stellar Evolution," in *Astrophysical Journal, 48.* (1918), pp. 35-49.

3. Jeans, James H. *Astronomy and Cosmogony, second edition.* (Cambridge, U. K.: Cambridge University Press, 1929), pp. 316-330.

4. *Ibid.*, p. 421.

5. *Ibid.*, p. 360.

6. Bondi, H. and Gold, T. "The Steady-State Theory of the Expanding Universe," in *Monthly Notices of the Royal Astronomical Society, 108.* (1948), pp. 252-270.

7. Hoyle, Fred. "A New Model for the Expanding Universe," in *Monthly Notices of the Royal Astronomical Society, 108.* (1948), pp. 372-382.

8. *Ibid.*, pp. 379-380.

9. Hoyle, Fred. "Stellar Evolution and the Expanding Universe," in *Nature, 163.* (1949), pp. 196-197.

10. Hoyle, Fred. "Development of the Universe," in *Nature, 165.* (1950), p. 68.

11. McCrea, W. H. "Relativity Theory and the Creation of Matter," in *Proceedings of the Royal Society of London, Series A, 206.* (1951), pp. 572-573.

References

12. Hoyle, Fred. "A New Model for the Expanding Universe," in *Monthly Notices of the Royal Astronomical Society, 108.* (1948), pp. 380.

13. Bondi, H. and Lyttleton, R. A. "On the Physical Consequences of a General Excess of Charge," in *Proceedings of the Royal Society of London, Series A, 252.* (1959), pp. 313-333.

14. Hoyle, Fred and Narlikar, J. V. "Mach's Principle and the Creation of Matter," in *Proceedings of the Royal Society of London, Series A, 273.* (1963), pp. 1-11.

15. Hoyle, Fred and Narlikar, J. V. "On the Avoidance of Singularities in C-field Cosmology," in *Proceedings of the Royal Society of London, Series A, 278.* (1964), pp. 465-478.

16. Hoyle, Fred and Narlikar, J. V. "On the Effects of the Non-Conservation of Baryons in Cosmology," in *Proceedings of the Royal Society of London, Series A, 290.* (1966), pp. 143-161.

17. Hoyle, Fred and Narlikar, J. V. "A Radical Departure from the 'Steady-State' Concept in Cosmology," in *Proceedings of the Royal Society of London, Series A, 290.* (1966), pp. 162-176.

18. Hoyle, Fred and Narlikar, J. V. "On the Formation of Elliptical Galaxies," in *Proceedings of the Royal Society of London, Series A, 290.* (1966), pp. 177-185.

19. Bondi, Herman. *Cosmology, second edition.* (Cambridge, United Kingdom: Cambridge University Press, 1960), p. 140.

20. Hoyle, Fred. "A New Model for the Expanding Universe," in *Monthly Notices of the Royal Astronomical Society, 108.* (1948), p. 372.

21. Hoyle, Fred. *The Nature of the Universe, second edition.* (Oxford, U. K.: Basil Blackwell, 1952), p. 109.

22. *Ibid.,* p. 111.

23. Hoyle, Fred. *Astronomy and Cosmology: a modern course.* (San Francisco: W. H. Freeman, 1975), pp. 684-685.

24. Hoyle, Fred. "The Universe: Past and Present Reflections," in *Annual Reviews of Astronomy and Astrophysics, 20.* (1982), p. 1.

25. *Ibid.,* p. 3.

26. Hoyle, Fred and Wickramasinghe, Chandra. *Evolution From Space.* (New York: Simon and Schuster, 1981), p. 143.

27. Hoyle, Fred. *Astronomy and Cosmology: a modern course.* (San Francisco: W. H. Freeman, 1975), p. 522.

28. Hoyle, Fred. "The Universe: Past and Present Reflections," in *Annual Reviews of Astronomy and Astrophysics, 20.* (1982), pp. 4-5.

29. Hoyle, Fred and Wickramasinghe, Chandra. *Evolution From Space.* (New York: Simon and Schuster, 1981), pp. 14-31, 129-143.

30. Thaxton, Charles B., Bradley, Walter L., and Olsen, Roger, L. *The Mystery of Life's Origin: Reassessing Current Theories.* (New York: Philosophical Library, 1984), pp. 2-179.

31. Kok, R. A., Taylor, J. A., and Bradley, W. L. "A Statistical Examination of Self-Ordering of Amino Acids in Proteins," in *Origins of Life and Evolution of the Biosphere, 18.* (1988), pp. 135-142.

32. Shapiro, Robert. *Origins: A Skeptic's Guide to the Creation of Life on Earth.* (New York: Summit Books, Simon & Schuster, 1986), pp. 117-131, 155-189.

33. Hoyle, Fred. "The Universe: Past and Present Reflections," in *Annual Reviews of Astronomy and Astrophysics, 20.* (1982), pp. 5-6.

34. Milne, E. A. "A Newtonian Expanding Universe," in *Quarterly Journal of Mathematics, Oxford Series, 5.* (1934), pp. 64-72.

35. McCrea, W. H. and Milne, E. A. "Newtonian Universes and the Curvature of Space," in *Quarterly Journal of Mathematics, Oxford Series, 5.* (1934), pp. 73-80.

36. Heckmann, O. and Schücking, E. "Bemerkungen zur Newtonschen Kosmologie. II," in *Zeitschrift für Astrophysik, 40.* (1956), pp. 81-92.

37. Novello, M. and Heintzmann, H. "An Eternal Universe," in *General Relativity and Gravitation, 16.* (1984), pp. 535-539.

NINE: Overthrow of Hesitation and Steady State

1. Mineur, Henri. "Sur les zéors des relations période-luminosité des Céphéides et des RR Lyrae," in *Académie des Sciences, Paris, Compte Rendu, 235.* (1952), pp. 1607-1608.

2. Humason, M. L., Mayall, N. U., and Sandage, A. R. "Redshifts and Magnitudes of Extragalactic Nebulae," in *Astronomical Journal, 61.* (1956), pp. 97-162.

3. Sandage, Allan. "The Redshift-Distance Relation: II The Hubble Diagram and Its Scatter for First-Ranked Cluster Galaxies: A Formal Value for q_o," in *Astrophysical Journal, 178.* (1972), pp. 1-24.

4. Sandage, Allan and Tammann, G. A. "Steps Toward the Hubble Constant. VIII. The Global Value," in *Astrophysical Journal, 256.* (1982), pp.339-345.

5. Sandage, Allan and Tammann, G. A. "The Dynamical Parameters of the Universe: H_o, q_o, Ω_o, Λ, and K," in *Large-Scale Structure of the Universe, Cosmology, and Fundamental Physics, Proceedings of the First ESO-CERN Symposium, CERN, Geneva, 21-25 Nov., 1983.* edited by G. Setti and L. Van Hove. (Geneva: CERN, 1984), pp. 127-149.

6. Sandage, Allan and Tammann, G. A. "The Hubble Constant as Derived from 21-cm Linewidths," in *Nature, 307.* (1984), pp. 326-329.

References

7. de Vaucouleurs, G. and Bollinger, G. "The Extragalactic Distance Scale. VII. The Velocity-Distance Relations in Different Directions and the Hubble Ratio Within and Without the Local Supercluster," in *Astrophysical Journal, 233*. (1979), pp. 433-452.

8. van den Bergh, Sidney. "Size and Age of the Universe," in *Science, 213*. (1981), pp. 825-830.

9. Madore, B. F. and Tully, R. B. (editors) "Proceedings of a NATO Advanced Research Workshop, Kailua Kona, Hawaii, Jan. 13-17, 1986," in *NATO Advanced Science Institutes, Series C: Mathematical and Physical Sciences, Vol 180*. (Dordrecht-Boston: D. Reidel, 1986).

10. van den Bergh, Sidney (editor). *The Extragalactic Distance Scale: Proceedings of the Astronomical Society of the Pacific 100th Anniversary Symposium, volume 4, held at Victoria, British Columbia, Canada, 1988*. (Provo, Utah: Brigham Young, 1989).

11. Sandage, Allan. "The Case for $H_0 \approx 55$ from the 21 Centimeter Linewidth Absolute Magnitude Relation for Field Galaxies," in *Astrophysical Journal, 331*. (1988), pp. 605-619.

12. Sandage, Allan. "A Case for $H_0 = 42$ and $\Omega_0 = 1$ Using Luminous Spiral Galaxies and the Cosmological Time Scale Test," in *Astrophysical Journal, 331*. (1988), pp. 583-604.

13. Sandage, Allan and Tammann, G. A. "The Hubble Constant from Pritchet and van den Bergh's Nova Distance to the Virgo Cluster," in *Astrophysical Journal, 328*. (1988), pp. 1-3.

14. Bottinelli, L., Gouguenheim, L., Paturel, G., and Teerikorpi, P. "The Malmquist Bias in the Extragalactic Distance Scale: Controversies and Misconceptions," in *Astrophysical Journal, 328*. (1988), pp. 4-22.

15. Tammann, Gustav A. "The Hubble Constant and the Deceleration Parameter," in *Proceedings of the International Astronomical Union Symposium No. 63: Confrontation of Cosmological Theories with Observational Data*, edited by M. S. Longair. (Dordrecht-Holland, Boston-USA: D. Reidel, 1974), pp. 47-59.

16. Vittorio, Nicola, Matarrese, Sabino, and Lucchin, Francesco. "Cold Dark Matter Dominated Inflationary Universe With $\Omega_o < 1$ and n < 1," in *Astrophysical Journal, 328*. (1988), pp. 69-76.

17. Peebles, P. J. E. "The Mean Mass Density of the Universe," in *Nature, 321*. (1986), pp. 27-32.

18. Hamilton, D. "The Spectral Evolution of Galaxies. I. an observational approach," in *Astrophysical Journal, 297*. (1985), pp. 371-389.

19. Steinhardt, Paul J. "Inflation and the Ω-Problem," in *Nature, 345*. (1990), pp. 47-49.

20. Petrosian, Vahé. "Confrontation of Lemaître Models and the Cosmological Constant with Observations," in *Proceedings of the I. A. U. Symposium No. 63: Confrontation of Cosmological Theories with Observational Data*, edited by M. S. Longair. (Dordrecht-Holland, Boston-U. S. A.: D. Reidel Publishing, 1974), pp. 31-46.

21. McCarthy, P. J., Dickinson, M., Filippenko, A. V., Spinrad, H., and van Breugel, W. J. M. "Serendipitous Discovery of a Redshift 4.4 QSO," in *Astrophysical Journal Letters, 328.* (1988), pp. L29-L33.

22. Warren, S. J., Hewett, P. C., Osmer, P. S., Irwin, M. J. "Quasars of Redshift z = 4.43 and z = 4.07 in the South Galactic Pole Field," in *Nature, 330.* (1987), pp. 453-455.

23. Schneider, Donald P., Schmidt, Maarten, and Gunn, James E. "PC 1158+4635: An Optically Selected Quasar with a Redshift of 4.73," in *Astronomical Journal, 98.* (1989), pp. 1951-1958.

24. Dunlop, J. S., Downes, A. J. B., Peacock, J. A., Savage, A., Lilly, S. J., Watson, F. G., and Longair, M. G. "Quasar with z = 3.71 and Limits on the Number of More Distant Objects," in *Nature, 319.* (1986), pp. 564-567.

25. Peterson, B. A., Savage, A., Jauncey, D. L., and Wright, A. E. "PKS 2000-330: A Quasi-Stellar Radio Source with a Redshift of 3.78," in *Astrophysical Journal Letters, 260.* (1982), pp. L27-L29.

26. Osmer, Patrick S. "Evidence for a Decrease in the Space Density of Quasars at z ≥ 3.5," in *Astrophysical Journal, 253.* (1982), pp. 28-37.

27. Schneider, Donald P., Schmidt, Maarten, and Gunn, James E. "Mapping the Quasar Cutoff Near Redshift 3.5 Using a Spectroscopic Transit Survey," in *Bulletin of the American Astronomical Society, 16.* (1984), p. 488.

28. Hazard, C., McMahon, R. G., and Sargent, W. L. W. "A QSO with Redshift 3.8 Found on a UK Schmidt Telescope IIIa-F Prism Plate," in *Nature, 322.* (1986), pp. 38-40.

29. Hazard, C. and McMahon, R. "New Quasars with z = 3.4 and 3.7 and the Surface Density of Very High Redshift Quasars," in *Nature, 314.* (1985), pp. 238-240.

30. Dolphin, Lambert T. *Jesus: Lord of Time and Space.* (Green Forest, AR: New Leaf Press, 1988).

31. Slusher, Harold S. *Age of the Cosmos.* (San Diego, CA: Institute for Creation Research, 1980).

32. Slusher, Harold S. *The Origin of the Universe, Revised Edition.* (El Cajon, California: Institute for Creation Research, 1980).

33. *Ibid.,* p. 14.

34. Setterfield, Barry. "The Velocity of Light and the Age of the Universe," in *Ex Nihilo, 1.* (1982), pp. 52-93.

35. Harris, David M. "A Solution to Seeing Stars," in *Creation Research Society Quarterly, 15.* (Sept. 1978), pp. 112-115.

36. Morton, Glenn R. "Electromagnetics and the Appearance of Age," in *Creation Research Society Quarterly, 18.* (Mar. 1982), pp. 227-232.

37. Norman, Trevor and Setterfield, Barry. "The Atomic Constants, Light, and Time," in *Stanford Research Institute International, Aug. 1987.*

References

38. Ross, Hugh. "Making Light of Apologetics," in *Facts & Faith, Vol. 1, No. 2,* 1987, pp. 1-2.

39. Fackerell, Edward D., "The Age of the Astronomical Universe," in *Ex Nihilo Technical Journal, 1.* (1984), pp. 87-94.

40. Zel'dovich, Ya. B. "The Theory of the Expanding Universe as Originated by A. A. Friedmann," in *Soviet Physics—Uspekhi, 6.* (1964), pp. 475-494.

41. Roberts, Morton S. "The Gaseous Content of Galaxies," in *International Astronomical Union Symposium No. 44, External Galaxies and Quasi-Stellar Objects,* edited by David S. Evans. (Dordrecht, Holland: D. Reidel, 1972), p. 33, fig. 19.

42. Sandage, Allan R., Tammann, G. A., and Hardy, Eduardo. "Limits on the Local Deviation of the Universe from a Homogeneous Model," in *Astrophysical Journal, 172.* (1972), pp. 253-263.

43. Sandage, A. R. and Hardy, E. "The Redshift-Distance Relation. VII. Absolute Magnitudes of the First Three Ranked Cluster Galaxies as Functions of Cluster Richness and Bautz-Morgan Cluster Type: The Effect of q_0," in *Astrophysical Journal, 183.* (1973), pp. 743-757.

44. Harkins, William D. "The Evolution of the Elements and the Stability of Complex Atoms," in *Journal of the American Chemical Society, 39.* (1917), pp. 856-879.

45. Tolman, Richard C. "Thermodynamic Treatment of the Possible Formation of Helium from Hydrogen," in *Journal of the American Chemical Society, 44.* (1922), pp. 1902-1908.

46. Alpher, Ralph A. and Herman, Robert C. "Theory of the Origin and Relative Abundance Distribution of the Elements," in *Reviews of Modern Physics, 22.* (1950), pp. 153-212.

47. Gamow, George. "Expanding Universe and the Origin of the Elements," in *Physical Review, 70.* (1946), pp. 572-573.

48. Alpher, Ralph A. and Herman, Robert C. "Evolution of the Universe," in *Nature, 162.* (1948), pp. 774-775.

49. Penzias, Arno A. and Wilson, Robert W. "A Measurement of Excess Antenna Temperature at 4080 Mc/s," in *Astrophysical Journal, 142.* (1965), pp. 419-421.

50. Dicke, R. H., Peebles, P. J. E., Roll, P. G., and Wilkinson, D. T. "Cosmic Black-Body Radiation," in *Astrophysical Journal, 142.* (1965), pp. 414-419.

51. Weiss, Rainer. "Measurements of the Cosmic Background Radiation," in *Annual Review of Astronomy and Astrophysics, 18.* (1980), pp. 489-535.

52. Smoot, George F. "Comments and Summary on the Cosmic Background Radiation," in *Proceedings of the International Astronomical Union Symposium, No. 104: Early Evolution of the Universe and its Present Structure,* ed. by G. O. Abell and G. Chincarini. (Dordrecht-Holland, Boston-U. S. A.: D. Reidel Publ., 1983), pp. 153-158.

53. Uson, Jaun M. and Wilkinson, David T. "Improved Limits on Small-Scale Anistropy in Cosmic Microwave Background," in *Nature, 312.* (1984), pp. 427-429.

54. Tayler, R. J. "The Origin of the Elements," in *Astrophysics,* edited by The Institute of Physics and the Physical Society. (New York: W. A. Benjamin, 1969), pp. 4-16.

55. Peebles, P. J. E. "Primeval Helium Abundance and Primeval Fireball," in *Physical Review Letters, 16.* (1966), pp. 410-413.

56. Peebles, P. J. E. *Physical Cosmology.* (Princeton, New Jersey: Princeton University Press, 1971), pp. 242-262.

57. Wagoner, Robert V., Fowler, William A., and Hoyle, Fred. "On the Synthesis of Elements at Very High Temperatures," in *Astrophysical Journal, 148.* (1967), pp. 3-49.

58. Peterson, I. "Cosmic Evidence of a Smooth Beginning," in *Science News, 137.* (1990), p. 36.

59. Peterson, I. "Cold Dark Matter Builds a Great Wall," in *Science News, 137.* (1990), p. 68.

60. Ross, Hugh. "Recent Refinements of the Big Bang," in *Facts & Faith, volume 4, number 1.* (1990), pp. 2-3.

61. Yang, J., Turner, M. S., Steigman, G., Schramm, D. N., and Olive, K. A. "Primordial Nucleosynthesis: A Critical Comparison of Theory and Observation," in *Astrophysical Journal, 281.* (1984), pp. 493-511.

62. Sandage, Allan and Tammann, G. A. "The Dynamical Parameters of the Universe: H_o, q_o, Ω_o, Λ, and K," in *Large-Scale Structure of the Universe, Cosmology, and Fundamental Physics, Proceedings of the First ESO-CERN Symposium, CERN, Geneva, 21-25 Nov., 1983,* ed. by G. Setti and L. Van Hove. (Geneva: CERN, 1984), pp. 134-139.

63. Petrosian, Vahé. "Confrontation of Lemaître Models and the Cosmological Constant with Observations," in *Proceedings of the I. A. U. Symposium No. 63: Confrontation of Cosmological Theories with Observational Data,* edited by M. S. Longair. (Dordrecht-Holland, Boston-U. S. A.: D. Reidel Publishing, 1974), pp. 34.

64. *Ibid.,* pp. 34-36.

65. Hawking, S. W. "The Cosmological Constant," in *Philosophical Transactions of the Royal Society of London, Series A, 310.* (1983), pp. 303-310.

66. Burbidge, E. M., Burbidge, G. R., Fowler, W. A., and Hoyle, F. "Synthesis of the Elements in Stars," in *Reviews of Modern Physics, 29.* (1957), pp. 547-650.

67. VandenBerg, D. A. "Star Clusters and Stellar Evolution. I. Improved Synthetic Color-Magnitude Diagrams for the Oldest Clusters," in *Astrophysical Journal Supplement, 51.* (1983), pp. 29-66.

References

68. Thielemann, F.-K., Metzinger, J., and Klapdor, H. V., "New Actinide Chronometer Production Ratios and the Age of the Galaxy," in *Astronomy and Astrophysics, 123*. (1983), pp. 162-169.

69. Fowler, W. A. "The Age of the Observable Universe," in *Quarterly Journal of the Royal Astronomical Society, 28*. (1987), pp. 87-108.

70. Cowan, John J., Thielemann, F.-K., and Truran, J. W., "Nuclear Chronometers from the r-Process and the Age of the Galaxy," in *Astrophysical Journal, 323*. (1987), pp. 543-552.

71. Clayton, Donald D. "Nuclear Cosmochronology within Analytic Models of the Chemical Evolution of the Solar Neighbourhood," in *Monthly Notices of the Royal Astronomical Society, 234*. (1988), pp. 1-36.

72. Cox, John P. and Giuli, R. Thomas. *Principles of Stellar Structure, Volume I: Physical Principles, Volume II: Applications to Stars.* (New York: Gordon and Breach, 1968).

73. Sandage, Allan. "The Oosterhoff Period Groups and the Age of Globular Clusters III. The Age of the Globular Cluster System," in *Astrophysical Journal, 252*. (1982), pp. 553-573.

74. VandenBerg, D. A. "Star Clusters and Stellar Evolution. I. Improved Synthetic Color-Magnitude Diagrams for the Oldest Clusters," in *Astrophysical Journal Supplement, 51*. (1983), pp. 29-66.

75. Hesser, James E., Harris, William E., Vandenberg, Don A., Allwright, J. W. B., Shott, Phillip, and Stetson, Peter B. "A CCD Color-Magnitude Study of 47 Tucanae," in *Publications of the Astronomical Society of the Pacific, 99*. (1987), pp. 739-808.

76. McClure, Robert D., Vandenberg, Don A., Bell, R. A., Hesser, James E., and Stetson, Peter B. "CCD Photometry of the Globular Cluster M68," in *Astronomical Journal, 93*. (1987), pp. 1144-1165.

77. Pilachowski, Catherine A. "The Abundance of Oxygen in M92 Giant Stars," in *Astrophysical Journal Letters, 326*. (1988), pp. L57-L60.

78. Bell, R. A. "Synthetic Strömgren Photometry for F Dwarf Stars," in *Astronomical Journal, 95*. (1988), pp. 1484-1493.

79. Hesser, James E. *et al*, p. 796.

80. Sandage, Allan and Tammann, G. A. "The Dynamical Parameters of the Universe: H_0, q_0, Ω_0, Λ, and K," in *Large-Scale Structure of the Universe, Cosmology, and Fundamental Physics, Proceedings of the First ESO-CERN Symposium, CERN, Geneva, 21-25 November, 1983*, edited by G. Setti and L. Van Hove. (Geneva: CERN, 1984), pp. 131.

81. Sandage, Allan. "A Case for $H_0 = 42$ and $\Omega_0 = 1$ Using Luminous Spiral Galaxies and the Cosmological Time Scale Test," *in Astrophysical Journal, 331*. (1988), p. 583.

82. Davidson, W. and Narlikar, J. V. "Cosmological Models and Their Observational Validation," in *Astrophysics: A Reprint from Reports on Progress in Physics*. (New York: W. A. Benjamin, 1969), pp.98-99, pp. 580-581 (original paper).

83. Peebles, P. J. E. "The Origin of Galaxies and Clusters of Galaxies," in *Science, 224.* (1984), pp. 1385-1391.

84. Woltjer, L. "Observational Evidence for the Evolution of the Universe," in *Large Scale Structure of the Universe, Cosmology and Fundamental Physics: ESO-CERN Symposium Proceedings,* edited by G. Setti and L. Van Hove. (Geneva: CERN, 1984), pp. 335-348.

85. Brecher, Kenneth and Silk, Joseph. "Lemaître Universe, Galaxy Formation and Observations," in *Astrophysical Journal, 158.* (1969), pp. 91-102.

TEN: Oscillating Universe

1. Gribbin, John. "Oscillating Universe Bounces Back," in *Nature, 259.* (1976), pp. 15-16.

2. de Sitter, Willem. "The Evolution of the Universe," in *Nature, 128.* (1931), p. 707.

3. Tolman, Richard C. "On the Problem of the Entropy of the universe as a Whole," in *Physical Review, 37.* (1931), pp. 1639-1660.

4. Tolman, Richard C. "Non-Static Model of Universe with Reversible Annihilation of Matter," in *Physical Review, 38.* (1931), pp. 797-814.

5. Tolman, Richard C. "Possibilities in Relativistic Thermodynamics for Irreversible Processes Without Exhaustion of Free Energy," in *Physical Review, 39.* (1932), pp. 320-336.

6. Tolman, Richard C. *Relativity, Thermodynamics, and Cosmology.* (Oxford, U. K.: Oxford University Press, 1934), §175.

7. Tolman, Richard C. "On the Theoretical Requirements for a Periodic Behavior of the Universe," in *Physical Review, 38.* (1931), pp. 1758-1771.

8. Tolman, Richard C. and Ward, Morgan. "On the Behavior of Non-Static Models of the Universe When the Cosmological Term is Omitted," in *Physical Review, 39.* (1932), p. 842.

9. Novikov, I. D. and Zel'dovich, Ya. B. "Physical Processes Near Cosmological Singularities," in *Annual Review of Astronomy and Astrophysics, 11.* (1973), pp. 387-412.

10. Landsberg, P. T. and Park, D. "Entropy in an Oscillating Universe," in *Proceedings of the Royal Society of London, Series A, 346.* (1975), pp. 485-495.

11. Novikov, I. D. and Zel'dovich, Ya. B., p. 402.

12. Dicke, R. H., Peebles, P. J. E., Roll, P. G., and Wilkinson, D. T. "Cosmic Black-Body Radiation," in *Astrophysical Journal Letters, 142.* (1965), pp. 414-419.

THE FINGERPRINT OF GOD

13. Penzias, A. A. and Wilson, R. W. "A Measurement of Excess Antenna Temperature at 4080 Mc/s," in *Astrophysical Journal Letters, 142.* (1965), pp. 419-421.

14. Dicke, R. H., Peebles, P. J. E., Roll, P. G., and Wilkinson, D. T., p. 414.

15. *Ibid.,* p. 415.

16. Peebles, P. J. E. "The Mean Density of the Universe," in *Nature, 321.* (1986), p.27.

17. Zwicky, Fritz. "Die Rotverschiebung von extragalaktischen Nebeln," in *Helvetica Physica Acta, 6.* (1933), pp. 110-127.

18. Zwicky, Fritz. "On the Masses of Nebulae and of Clusters of Nebulae," in *Astrophysical Journal, 86.* (1937), pp. 217-246.

19. Gott III, Richard J., Gunn, James E., Schramm, David N., and Tinsley, Beatrice M. "An Unbound Universe?" in *Astrophysical Journal, 194.* (1974), pp. 543-553.

20. Spinrad, Hyron and Djorgovski, S. "The Status of the Hubble Diagram in 1986," in *Observational Cosmology, Proceedings of the 124th Symposium of the International Astronomical Union, held in Beijing, China, Aug. 25-30, 1986* (ed.: Hewitt, A., Burbidge, G., and Fang, L. Z.), (Dordrecht-Boston: D. Reidel, 1987), pp. 129-141.

21. Steinhardt, Paul J. "Inflation and the Ω-Problem," in *Nature, 345.* (1990), pp. 47-49.

22. Peebles, P. J. E. "The Mean Mass Density of the Universe," in *Nature, 321.* (1986), pp. 27-32.

23. Hamilton, Donald. "The Spectral Evolution of Galaxies. I. An Observational Approach," in *Astrophysical Journal, 297.* (1985), pp. 371-389.

24. Sandage, Allan and Tammann, G. A. "The Dynamical Parameters of the Universe: H_o, q_o, Ω_o, Λ, and K," in *Large-Scale Structure of the Universe, Cosmology, and Fundamental Physics, Proceedings of the First ESO-CERN Symposium, CERN, Geneva, 21-25 Nov., 1983,* edited by G. Setti and L. van Hove. (Geneva: CERN, 1984), pp. 127-149.

25. Yang, J., Turner, M. S., Steigman, G., Schramm, D. N., and Olive, K. A. "Primordial Nucleosynthesis: a critical comparison of theory and observation," in *Astrophysical Journal, 281.* (1984), pp. 493-511.

26. Uson, Juan M. and Wilkinson, David T. "Improved Limits on Small-Scale Anistropy in Cosmic Microwave Background," in *Nature, 312.* (1984), pp. 427-429.

27. Ellis, G. F. R. "Does Inflation Necessarily Imply $\Omega = 1$?" in *Classical and Quantum Gravity, 5.* (1988), pp. 891-901.

28. Guth, Alan H. "Inflationary Universe: A Possible Solution to the Horizon and Flatness Problems," in *Physical Review D, 23.* (1981), pp. 347-356.

29. Nanopoulos, D. V. "The Inflationary Universe," in *Comments on Astrophysics, 10.* (1985), pp. 224-226.

205

30. Novikov, I. D. and Zel'dovich, Ya. B., p. 401.

31. Guth, Alan H. and Sher, Marc. "The Impossibility of a Bouncing Universe," in *Nature, 302.* (1983), pp. 505-507.

32. Bludman, Sidney A. "Thermodynamics and the End of a Closed Universe," in *Nature, 308.* (1984), pp. 319-322.

ELEVEN: Transcendence and Quantum Gravity

1. Harrison, E. R. "Standard Model of the Early Universe," in *Annual Review of Astronomy and Astrophysics, 11.* (1973), pp. 155-186.

2. Weinberg, Steven. *The First Three Minutes: A Modern View of the Origin of the Universe.* (New York: Basic Books, 1977).

3. Silk, Joseph. *The Big Bang.* (San Francisco: W. H. Freeman, 1980).

4. Guth, Alan H. "Inflationary Universe: A Possible Solution to the Horizon and Flatness Problems," in *Physical Review D, 23.* (1981), pp. 347-356.

5. Barrow, J. D. and Turner, M. S. "The Inflationary Universe—Birth, Death, and Transfiguration," in *Nature, 298.* (1982), pp. 801-805.

6. Linde, A. D. "The Present Status of the Inflationary Universe Scenario," in *Comments on Astrophysics, 10.* (1985), pp. 229-237.

7. Tolman, Richard C. and Ward, Morgan. "On the Behavior of Non-Static Models of the Universe When the Cosmological Term is Omitted," in *Physical Review, 39.* (1932), p. 842.

8. Barrow, John D. and Silk, Joseph. *The Left Hand of Creation: The Origin and Evolution of the Expanding Universe.* (New York, Basic Books, 1983), p. 32.

9. Davies, Paul. *God and the New Physics.* (New York, Simon & Schuster, 1983), p. 56.

10. Pagels, Heinz R. *Perfect Symmetry: The Search for the Beginning of Time.* (New York: Simon & Schuster, 1985), p. 243.

11. Hawking, Stephen W. and Ellis, George F. R. "The Cosmic Black-Body Radiation and the Existence of Singularities in our Universe," in *Astrophysical Journal, 152.* (1968), pp. 25-36.

12. Hawking, Stephen and Penrose, Roger. "The Singularities of Gravitational Collapse and Cosmology," in *Proceedings of the Royal Society of London, Series A, 314.* (1970), pp. 529-548.

13. Barrow, John D. and Silk, Joseph, pp. 38-39.

14. Brans, C. and Dicke, R. H. "Mach's Principle and a Relativistic Theory of Gravitation," in *Physical Review, 124*. (1961), pp. 925-935.

15. Moffat, J. W. "Consequences of a New Experimental Determination of the Quadrupole Moment of the Sun for Gravitation Theory," in *Physical Review Letters, 50*. (1983), pp. 709-712.

16. Ellis, George F. R. "Alternatives to the Big Bang," in *Annual Reviews of Astronomy and Astrophysics, 22*. (1984), pp. 157-184.

17. Boslough, John. "Inside the Mind of a Genius," in *Reader's Digest, February 1984*, p. 120.

18. Pagels, Heinz R., p. 244.

19. Tryon, Edward P. "Is the Universe a Vacuum Fluctuation," in *Nature, 246*. (1973), pp. 396-397.

20. Atkatz, D. and Pagels, H. "Origin of the Universe as a Quantum Tunneling Event," in *Physical Review D, 25*. (1982), pp. 2065-2073.

21. Vilenkin, Alexander. "Creation of Universes from Nothing," in *Physical Letters B, 117*. (1982), pp. 25-28.

22. Zel'dovich, Yakob B. and Grishchuk, L. P. "Structure and Future of the 'New' Universe," in *Monthly Notices of the Royal Astronomical Society, 207*. (1984), pp. 23P-28P.

23. Vilenkin, Alexander. "Birth of Inflationary Universes," in *Physical Review D, 27*. (1983), pp. 2848-2855.

24. Vilenkin, Alexander. "Quantum Creation of Universes," in *Physical Review D, 30*. (1984), pp. 509-511.

25. Hartle, James B. and Hawking Steven W. "Wave Function of the Universe," in *Physical Review D, 28*. (1983), pp. 2960-2975.

26. Hawking, Steven W. "The Quantum State of the Universe," in *Nuclear Physics B, 239*. (1984), pp. 257-276.

27. Pagels, Heinz R., p. 347.

28. Hawking, Stephen W. *A Brief History of Time: From the Big Bang to Black Holes*. (New York: Bantam Books, 1988), p. 139.

29. II Timothy 1:9 and Titus 1:2, *The Holy Bible, New International Version*.

30. Hawking, Stephen W., p. 141.

31. Adler, Jerry; Lubenow, Gerald C.; and Malone, Maggie. "Reading God's Mind," in *Newsweek, June 13*. (1988), p. 59.

32. Jaki, Stanley L. *Cosmos and Creator*. (Edinburgh, U. K.: Scottish Academic Press, 1980), pp. 49-54.

33. Brout, R., Englert, F., and Gunzig, E. in *Annales de Physiques, 115*. (1978), pp. 78-80.

34. Brout, R., Englert, F., and Spindel, P. "Cosmological Origin of the Grand-Unification Mass Scale," in *Physical Review Letters, 43*. (1979), pp. 417-420.

35. Gott III, J. Richard. "Creation of Open Universes from de Sitter Space," in *Nature, 295.* (1982), pp. 304-307.

36. Gott III, J. Richard, p. 306.

37. Davies, Paul. *God and the New Physics.* (New York: Simon and Schuster, 1983), pp. 25-43, specifically pp. 38-39.

38. Taubes, Gary. "Everything's Now Tied to Strings," in *Discover, volume 7, November, 1986.* pp. 34-56.

39. Davies, Paul. *Superforce: The Search for a Grand Unified Theory of Nature.* (New York: Simon and Schuster, 1984), p. 243.

TWELVE: Design and the Anthropic Principle

1. Wheeler, John A. "Foreword," in *The Anthropic Cosmological Principle* by John D. Barrow and Frank J. Tipler. (Oxford, U. K.: Clarendon Press, 1986), p. vii.

2. Franz, Marie-Louise. *Patterns of Creativity Mirrored in Creation Myths.* (Zurich: Spring, 1972).

3. Kilzhaber, Albert R. *Myths, Fables, and Folktales.* (New York: Holt, 1974), pp. 113-114.

4. Dirac, P. A. M. "The Cosmological Constants," in *Nature 139.* (1937), p. 323.

5. Dicke, Robert H. "Dirac's Cosmology and Mach's Principle," in Nature, 192. (1961), pp. 440-441.

6. Guth, A. H. "Inflationary Universe: a possible solution to the horizon and flatness problems," in *Physical Review D, 23.* (1981), p. 348.

7. Carr, B. J. and Rees, M. J. "The Anthropic Principle and the Structure of the Physical World," in *Nature, 278.* (1979), p. 610.

8. Barrow, John D. and Tipler, Frank J. *The Anthropic Cosmological Principle.* (New York: Oxford University Press, 1986), pp. 401-402.

9. Trefil, James S. *The Moment of Creation.* (New York: Scribner's Sons, 1983), pp. 141-142.

10. Hoyle, Fred. Galaxies, Nuclei, and Quasars. (New York: Harper and Row, 1965), pp. 147-150.

11. Hoyle, Fred. "The Universe: Past and Present Reflections," in *Annual Review of Astronomy and Astrophysics, 20.* (1982), p. 16.

12. Greenstein, George. *The Symbiotic Universe: Life and Mind in the Cosmos.* (New York: William Morrow, 1988), pp. 26-27.

13. Shklovskii, I. S. and Sagan, Carl. *Intelligent Life in the Universe*. (San Francisco: Holden-Day, 1966), pp. 343-350.

14. *Ibid.*, p. 413.

15. Rood, Robert T. and Trefil, James S. *Are We Alone? The Possibility of Extraterrestrial Civilizations*. (New York: Scribner's Sons, 1983).

16. Barrow, John D. and Tipler, Frank J., pp. 510-575.

17. Anderson, Don L. "The Earth as a Planet: Paradigms and Paradoxes," in *Science, 223*. (1984), pp. 347-355.

18. Campbell, I. H. and Taylor, S. R. "No Water, No Granite—No Oceans, No Continents," in *Geophysical Research Letters, 10*. (1983), pp. 1061-1064.

19. Carter, Brandon. "The Anthropic Principle and Its Implications for Biological Evolution," in *Philosophical Transactions of the Royal Society of London, Series A, 310*. (1983), pp. 352-363.

20. Hammond, Allen H. "The Uniqueness of the Earth's Climate," in *Science, 187*. (1975), p. 245.

21. Toon, Owen B. and Olson, Steve. "The Warm Earth," in *Science 85, October*. (1985), pp. 50- 57.

22. Gale, George. "The Anthropic Principle," in *Scientific American, 245, No. 6*. (1981), pp. 154-171.

23. Ross, Hugh. *Genesis One: A Scientific Perspective*. (Pasadena, California: Reasons to Believe, 1983), pp. 6-7.

24. Cottrell, Ron. *The Remarkable Spaceship Earth*. (Denver, Colorado: Accent Books, 1982).

25. Ter Harr, D. "On the Origin of the Solar System," in *Annual Review of Astronomy and Astrophysics, 5*. (1967), pp. 267-278.

26. Greenstein, George., pp. 68-97.

27. Templeton, John M. "God Reveals Himself in the Astronomical and in the Infinitesimal," in *Journal of the American Scientific Affiliation, December 1984*. (1984), pp. 196-198.

28. Hart, Michael H. "The Evolution of the Atmosphere of the Earth," in *Icarus, 33*. (1978), pp. 23-39.

29. Hart, Michael H. "Habitable Zones about Main Sequence Stars," in *Icarus, 37*. (1979), pp. 351-357.

30. Owen, Tobias; Cess, Robert D.; and Ramanathan, V. "Enhanced CO_2 Greenhouse to Compensate for Reduced Solar Luminosity on Early Earth," in *Nature, 277*. (1979), pp. 640-641.

31. Ward, William R. "Comments on the Long-Term Stability of the Earth's Obliquity," in *Icarus, 50*. (1982), pp. 444-448.

32. Gribbin, John. "The Origin of Life: Earth's Lucky Break," in *Science Digest, May 1983*. (1983), pp. 36-102.

33. Tipler, Frank J. reviewing "The Search for Extraterrestrial Life: Recent Developments," in *Physics Today, 40*, December 1987, p. 92.

34. Davies, Paul. *The Cosmic Blueprint*. (New York: Simon and Schuster, 1988), p. 203.
35. Wheeler, John Archibald. "Bohr, Einstein, and the Strange Lesson of the Quantum," in *Mind in Nature*, edited by Richard Q. Elvee. (New York: Harper and Row, 1981), p. 18.
36. Greenstein, George., p. 223.
37. Herbert, Nick. *Quantum Reality: Beyond the New Physics*. (New York: Anchor Books, Doubleday, 1987), in particular pp. 16-29.
38. Jaki, Stanley L. Cosmos and Creator. (Edinburgh, U. K.: Scottish Academic Press, 1980), pp. 96-98.
39. Trefil, James S., pp. 91-101.
40. Barrow, John D. and Tipler, Frank J. *The Anthropic Cosmological Principle*. (New York: Oxford University Press, 1986).
41. *Ibid.*, p. 677.
42. *Ibid.*, pp. 677, 682.
43. Gardner, Martin. "WAP, SAP, PAP, and FAP." in *The New York Review of Books, 23, May 8, 1986, No. 8.* (1986), pp. 22-25.
44. *The Holy Bible, New International Version*. Colossians 2:8.
45. Cairns, John; Overbaugh, Julie; and Miller, Stephan. "The Origin of Mutants," in *Nature, 335.* (1988), pp. 142-145.
46. Stolzenburg, W. "Hypermutation: Evolutionary fast track?" in *Science News, 137.* (1990), p. 391.
47. Hall, Barry G. "Adaptive Evolution that Requires Multiple Spontaneous Mutations. I. Mutations Involving an Insertion Sequence," in *Genetics, 120.* (1988), pp. 887-897.
48. Thaxton, Charles B., Bradley, Walter L., and Olsen, Roger. *The Mystery of Life's Origin*. (New York: Philosophical Library, 1984), pp. 15, 44, 76-94.
49. Yockey, Hubert P. "On the Information Content of Cytochrome c," in *Journal of Theoretical Biology, 67.* (1977), pp. 345-376.
50. Yockey, Hubert P. "Self Organization Origin of Life Scenarios and Information Theory," in *Journal of Theoretical Biology, 91.* (1981), pp. 13-31.
51. Lake, James A. "Evolving Ribosome Structure: Domains in Archaebacteria, Eubacteria, Eocytes, and Eukaryotes," in *Annual Review of Biochemistry, 54.* (1985), pp. 507-530.
52. Dufton, M. J. "Genetic Code Redundancy and the Evolutionary Stability of Protein Secondary Structure," in *Journal of Theoretical Biology, 116.* (1985), pp. 343-348.
53. Yockey, Hubert P. "Do Overlapping Genes Violate Molecular Biology and the Theory of Evolution," in *Journal of Theoretical Biology, 80.* (1979), pp. 21-26.

54. Abelson, John. "RNA Processing and the Intervening Sequence Problem," in *Annual Review of Biochemistry, 48.* (1979), pp. 1035-1069.

55. Hinegardner, Ralph T. and Engleberg, Joseph. "Rationale for a Universal Genetic Code," in *Science, 142.* (1963), pp. 1083-1085.

56. Neurath, Hans. "Protein Structure and Enzyme Action," in *Reviews of Modern Physics, 31.* (1959), pp. 185-190.

57. Hoyle, Fred and Wickramasinghe, Chandra. *Evolution From Space.* (New York: Simon and Schuster, 1981), pp. 14-97.

58. Thaxton, Charles B., Bradley, Walter L., and Olsen, Roger. *The Mystery of Life's Origin.* (New York: Philosophical Library, 1984).

59. Shapiro, Robert. *Origins: A Skeptic's Guide to the Creation of Life on Earth.* (New York: Summit Books, 1986), 117-131.

60. Ross, Hugh., pp. 9-10.

61. Yockey, Hubert P. "A Calculation of the Probability of Spontaneous Biogenesis by Information Theory," in *Journal of Theoretical Biology, 67.* (1977), pp. 377-398.

62. Duley, W. W. "Evidence Against Biological Grains in the Interstellar Medium," in *Quarterly Journal of the Royal Astronomical Society, 25.* (1984), pp. 109-113.

63. Kok, Randall A., Taylor, John A., and Bradley, Walter L. "A Statistical Examination of Self-Ordering of Amino Acids in Proteins," in *Origins of Life and Evolution of the Biosphere, 18.* (1988), pp. 135-142.

64. Shklovskii, Iosef, and Sagan, Carl. *Intelligent Life in the Universe.* (San Francisco: Holden-Day, 1966), pp. 207-211.

65. Hoyle, Fred, and Wickramasinghe, Chandra. *Evolution from Space.* (New York: Simon and Schuster, 1981), pp. 39-61.

66. Eberhart, Jonathan. "Have Earth Rocks Gone To Mars?" in *Science News, 135.* (1989), p. 191.

THIRTEEN: Biblical Evidence for Long Creation Days

1. Free, Joseph. *Archaeology and Bible History.* (Wheaton, Illinois: Victor Books, 1950), p. 50.

2. Augustine. "The Literal Meaning of Genesis, Books Four and Five," in *Ancient Christian Writers: The Works of the Fathers in Translation,* edited by Johannes Quasten, Walter J. Burghardt, and Thomas Comerford Lawler. Number 41, St. Augustine, The Literal Meaning of Genesis. translated and annotated by John Hammond Taylor. Vol. I, Books 1 - 6. (New York: Newman Press, 1982), pp. 133-148.

3. Augustine. "The Confessions, Book XIII, chapters 48-52," in *Great Books of the Western World, volume 18, Augustine.* edited by Robert Maynard Hutchins. (Chicago: Encyclopædia Britannica, 1952), p. 124.

4. Augustine. "The City of God, Book XI, chapters 7-8, 30-31" in *Great Books of the Western World, volume 18, Augustine,* edited by Robert Maynard Hutchins. (Chicago: Encyclopædia Britannica, 1952), pp. 326, 339-340.

5. Aquinas, Thomas. *Basic Writings of Saint Thomas Aquinas, Volume One,* edited and annotated by Anton C. Pegis. (New York: Random House, 1945), pp. 680-681.

6. North, Gary. *The Dominion Covenant: Genesis.* (Tyler, Texas: Institute for Christian Economics, 1987), pp. 254-255.

7. Whitcomb Jr., John C. *The Early Earth.* (Grand Rapids, Michigan: Baker Book House, 1972), pp. 29-37 and references therein.

8. Whitcomb, John C. and DeYoung, Donald B. *The Moon: Its Creation, Form, and Significance.* (Winona Lake, Indiana: BMH Books, 1978), p. 69.

9. Morris, Henry. "The Compromise Road," in *Impact, No. 177* (March 1988), p. iv.

10. North, Gary., p. 417.

11. Psalm 119:160, Titus 1:2, Hebrews 6:18. *The Holy Bible, New International Version.*

12. Genesis 1:1, Hebrews 11:3. *The Holy Bible, New International Version.*

13. II Timothy 3:16. *The Holy Bible, New International Version.*

14. Harris, R. Laird, Archer, Gleason L., and Waltke, Bruce K. *Theological Wordbook of the Old Testament, Volume II.* Chicago: Moody Press, 1980), pp. 672-673.

15. Tregelles, Samuel P. *Gesenius' Hebrew-Chaldee Lexicon to the Old Testament.* (Grand Rapids, Michigan: Baker Book House, 1979), pp. 612-613.

16. Raloff, Janet. "Earth Day 1980: The 29th Day?" in *Science News, 117.* (1980), p. 270.

17. Lewin Roger. "No Dinosaurs This Time," in *Science, 221.* (1983), p. 1169.

18. Ehrlich, Paul R.,Ehrlich, Anne H., and Holdren, J. P. *Ecoscience: Population, Resources, Environment.* (San Francisco: W. H. Freeman, 1977), p. 142.

19. Ehrlich, Paul R. and Ehrlich, Anne H. *Extinction: The Causes and Consequences of the Disappearance of Species.* (New York: Ballantine, 1981), p. 33.

20. Ehrlich, Paul R. and Ehrlich, Anne H., p. 23.

21. Harris, R. Laird, Archer, Gleason L., and Waltke, Bruce K. *Theological Wordbook of the Old Testament, Volume I.* Chicago: Moody Press, 1980), pp. 378-379.

22. Archer, Gleason L. "A Response to The Trustworthiness of Scripture in Areas Relating to Natural Science," in *Hermeneutics, Inerrancy, and the Bible.* edited by Earl D. Radmacher and Robert D. Preus. (Grand Rapids, Michigan: Academie Books, 1986), pp. 329.

23. Jacobs, J. A., Russell, R. D., and Tuzo Wilson, J. *Physics and Geology.* (New York: McGraw-Hill, 1959), p. 135.

24. LaBonte, Barry and Howard, Robert. *Science, 214.* (1981), pp. 907-909.

25. Bower, Bruce. "Retooled Ancestors," in *Science News, 133.* (1988), pp. 344-345.

26. Bower, Bruce. "Early Human Skelton Apes Its Ancestors," in *Science News, 131.* (1987), p. 340.

27. Bower, Bruce. "Family Feud: Enter the 'Black Skull,'" in *Science News, 131.* (1987), pp. 58-59.

28. Simon, C., "Stone-Age Sanctuary, Oldest Known Shrine, Discovered in Spain," in *Science News, 120.* (1981), p. 357.

29. Bower, Bruce. "When the Human Spirit Soared," in *Science News, 130.* (1986), pp. 378-379.

30. Jones, J. S. and Rouhani, S., "Human Evolution: How small was the bottleneck?" in *Nature, 319.* (1986), pp. 449-450.

31. Bower, Bruce. "Retooled Ancestors," in *Science News, 133.* (1988), pp. 344-345.

32. Bower, Bruce. "Early Human Skelton Apes Its Ancestors," in *Science News, 131.* (1987), p. 340.

33. Lewin, Roger. "Unexpected Anatomy in Homo erectus," in *Science, 226.* (1984), p. 529.

FOURTEEN: Genesis Creation Account

1. Simpson, D. C. *Penteteuchal Criticism.* (London, U. K.: Oxford University Press, Humphrey Milford, 1924), pp. 23-24.

2. Green, William Henry. *The Higher Criticism of the Pentateuch.* (New York: Charles Scribner's Sons, 1895), p. 61.

3. Osgood, Howard. "Jean Astruc," in *Presbyterian and Reformed Review, 3.* (1892), pp. 97-101.

4. *Ibid.,* p. 87.

5. Astruc, Jean. *Conjectures sur les mémoirs originaux dont il parait que Moise s'est servi pour composer la Genèse, avec des remarques qui appuient ou éclaircissens ces conjectures.* (Bruxelles, Fricx, 1753), pp. 378, 439.

6. O'Doherty, Eamonn. "The Conjectures of Jean Astruc, 1753," in *Catholic Biblical Quarterly, 15.* (1953), pp. 300-304.

7. Eichhorn, Johann Gottfried. *Einleitung in das Alte Testament, volumes 1 - 5.* (Göttingen, Netherlands: C. E. Rosenbusch, 1823-24). [Most of the relevant material is in the first volume.]

8. Driver, S. R. *The Book of Genesis, third edition.* (London, U. K.: Methuen and Co., 1904), pp. 3-43.

9. Buttrick, George A.; Bowie, Walter R.; Scherer, Paul; Knox, John; Terrien, Samuel; and Harmon, Nolan B. (editors) *The Interpreter's Bible, volume 1.* (New York: Abingdon Press, 1952), pp. 462-500.

10. Berkhof, L. *Systematic Theology, fourth edition.* (Grand Rapids, Michigan: William B. Eerdmans, 1941), pp. 150-160.

11. Green, William Henry. *The Unity of the Book of Genesis.* (New York: Charles Scribner's Sons, 1897), pp. 25-26.

12. Keil, C. F. and Delitzsch, F. *Biblical Commentary on the Old Testament, volume 1, The Pentateuch,* translated from the German by James Martin. (Grand Rapids, Michigan: Wm. B. Eerdmans, 1949), pp. 87.

13. Redpath, Henry A. *Modern Criticism and the Book of Genesis.* (London, U. K.: Society for Promoting Christian Knowledge, 1905), p. 19.

14. Keil, Karl Friedrich. *Manual of Historico-Critical Introduction to the Canonical Scriptures of the Old Testament, volume 1,* translated from the second edition by George C. M. Douglas. (Grand Rapids, Michigan: Wm. B. Eerdmans, 1952), p. 104.

15. Harris, R. Laird, Archer, Gleason J., Waltke, Bruce K. *Theological Wordbook of the Old Testament, volume 2.* (Chicago: Moody Press, 1980), p. 935.

16. Driver, S. R., p. 3.

17. Harris, R. Laird, Archer, Gleason J., Waltke, Bruce K. *Theological Wordbook of the Old Testament, volume 1.* (Chicago: Moody Press, 1980), p. 127.

18. Driver, S. R., p. 5.

19. Ross, Hugh. *Genesis One: A Scientific Perspective.* (P.O. 5978, Pasadena, California 91117: Reasons To Believe, 1983).

Glossary

accretion disks A disk of material (gases, ices, dust, rocks, etc.) surrounding a star or stellar object in which matter is being gathered and condensed.

adiabatic expansion A volume increase wherein cooling results from the expansion alone, not from any loss of energy from the system.

agnostism Belief that the existence of a divine being cannot be proved.

albedo The ratio of reflected light to the total amount of light falling on a surface.

amino acids Organic molecules containing the amino group NH_2 and at least one carboxyl group. These acids form the basic constituents of all proteins.

amino acid residues The essential molecular building blocks within proteins.

angular momentum The measure of a body's tendency to continue rotating about its axis.

anthropic principle The observation that the universe has all the necessary and narrowly-defined characteristics to make man and his sustained existence possible.

antinomy A contradiction or inconsistency between two apparently reasonable statements or principles.

appearance of age The hypothesis that God created the universe, the earth, and life with (false) indicators of a nonexistent past. If this hypothesis were true, scientific measurements of great age conceivably could be reconciled with a recent-creation interpretation of certain biblical passages.

atheist Someone who denies the existence of a divine being.

axiom A self-evident proposition; a statement that needs no proof because its truth is considered obvious.

baryons (also known as nucleons) The heavier particles, e.g. protons and neutrons, that make up the nucleus of an atom; any particle whose decay products include a proton.

beauty principle The proposition that the correct description of nature is that which manifests the greatest degree of simplicity, elegance, harmony, and consistency.

big bang (inflationary) The theory that the universe expands adiabatically according to the standard equations of general relativity from an initial state of infinite density, temperature, and pressure *except* during the period from about 10^{-43} to 10^{-34} seconds (of the universe's existence), when it expanded at an exponentionally accelerated rate.

big bang (standard) The theory that the universe expands adiabatically according to the standard equations of general relativity from an initial state of infinite density, temperature, and pressure.

bipedal Characteristically walking on two feet.

black body radiation Radiation characteristic of a body that perfectly absorbs all the radiation falling on it.

black hole A massive system so centrally condensed that its force of gravity prevents everything within it, including light, from escaping.

closed universe An expanding universe with sufficient density that gravity eventually halts the expansion and forces a collapse.

continuous creation The hypothesis that everywhere in the universe new matter is spontaneously and continuously being created out of nothing. In steady state theories the rate of creation is set so that, as the universe expands, its overall density remains a constant.

corollary A proposition logically derived from another that already has been proved.

cosmic rays Streams of penetrating particles that bombard the earth from outer space. The most energetic of these particles come primarily from supernova remnants.

cosmological constant (Λ) The term expressing a hypothesized repulsive force. Einstein added it to his original gravitational theory to enable the theory to predict a static, non-expanding universe. There is no evidence, as yet, to support the existence of such a force.

cosmology   The study of the universe as a whole—its structure, characteristics, origin, and development.

coupling constant   A number that expresses how strongly any force interacts between two bodies.

critical density   An average density (of the universe) that if exceeded will cause an eventual collapse of the universe. Alexander Friedmann calculated that figure to be about 2×10^{-29} grams/cubic centimeter.   An average density of that value or less means that the universe will continue to expand.

deceleration parameter (q_o)   The term expressing the rate by which the expansion of the universe slows down.

deist   Someone who believes in the existence of a divine being, but a distant one, a deity who maintains no personal interaction with the creatures he caused to come into existence.

de Sitter universe   A model of the universe that appears static because of a peculiar system of spatial coordinates and the assumption that the matter content of the universe is zero. When the assumption that the universe contains zero matter is corrected, the model predicts an expanding universe.

deuterium   A heavy isotope of hydrogen with one neutron and one proton in the nucleus.

deoxyribonucleic acid (DNA)   A long double strand of nucleotides containing the genetic code that specifies and controls all the characteristics of an organism.

electron   The lightest of the elementary particles that have measurable mass.   It carries a negative charge.

entropy   A measure of the amount of energy in a disordered form (i.e. unavailable for work) within a system.

enzymes   Protein-like molecules that serve as catalysts.

evolution   A process of gradual development; change taking place through time.

evolutionism   The belief that atoms can assemble themselves into advanced life forms by natural processes alone, i.e. without input from a divine designer.

flat universe   A universe with a density equal to Friedmann's critical value, a universe expanding forever at a rate just fast enough to prevent collapse.

frame of reference The position in time and space from which measurements and observations are made.

frequency For any kind of wave, the time between peaks of successive wave crests.

fundamentalism A movement that arose at the beginning of the 20th century to reaffirm the tenets of orthodox Protestant Christianity and to defend the Faith militantly against the challenges of liberal theology, higher criticism, and Darwinism.

general revelation God's expression of Himself to man through the realm of nature.

genome The complete set of chromosomes necessary for reproduction.

globular cluster A spherically symmetric system of stars typically containing over 100,000 stars.

gravitational collapse or contraction The falling of matter toward the center of a system as a result of mutual gravitational attraction.

greenhouse effect The retention of heat at the earth's surface caused by atmospheric gases such as carbon dioxide that allow short wavelength radiation from the sun to pass through but then trap the long wavelength radiation emitted by the earth.

half-life The time required for the disintegration of half the atoms in a sample of a radioactive isotope of an element.

heliocentrism The belief that the sun is the center of the solar system.

hesitation model A model for the universe wherein the value for the cosmological constant is carefully set so that the expansion of the universe can be slowed down for an arbitrary period.

higher criticism Application of the methods and suppositions of literary and form criticism to the study of the Bible.

hominid Any primate species that bears a close anatomical resemblence and some behavioral resemblence to modern man.

homogeneous A system in which the component parts are identical in their structure and characteristics.

Hubble age The age of the universe calculated by extrapolating the observed expansion of the universe backward in time to the starting point.

Glossary

Hubble's constant   The observed expansion rate of the universe.

incompleteness theorem   A principle derived by Kurt Gödel which states that with incomplete information about a system, it is impossible to prove a necessarily true theorem (i.e. a one and only one descriptive statement) about that system.

isotope   One of two or more forms of the same element with different atomic weights, i.e. with different numbers of neutrons.

isotropic   Independent of direction or angle.   A property is isotropic if it is the same when viewed from any direction.

leptons   Elementary particles which do not participate in strong nuclear reactions, e.g. electrons, neutrinos, and photons.

light year   The distance light travels in one year (approximately 5.9 trillion miles or 9.5 trillion kilometers).

luminosity   A measure of the intensity of light emitted by an object.

microwave background   The radiation left over from the big bang.   This radiation follows the spectrum of a black body radiator with a temperature of about 3° Kelvin.

missing mass   The amount of mass, beyond what has been measured, that would be required to eventually bring the universe collapsing in on itself.

nebular hypothesis   The idea that the galaxies, stars, and planets all condensed out of an amorphous nebula of molecules and dust.

neo-Darwinian evolution   The hypothesis that all life forms developed by natural processes alone from atoms to molecules to proteins to cells to advanced organisms.

neutrinos   A class of electrically neutral particles, with little or no mass, which experience weak-nuclear and gravitational interactions only.

neutron   An electrically neutral elementary particle with a large mass; one of the class of particles known as baryons.

non-theist   Someone who does not acknowledge the reality of God.

nuclear fusion   The merging of lightweight atomic nuclei into more massive nuclei.   A small amount of the combined mass is lost because it is converted into energy.

nucleochronology The age-dating of astronomical bodies from the relative abundances of radioactive isotopes.

nucleosynthesis The process of forming elements from protons and neutrons.

Olber's paradox The question, "Why is the night sky dark if the universe is infinitely large, infinitely old, with an infinite number of stars?"

open universe A universe with a density less than (or equal to) Friedmann's critical value. Gravity cannot prevent such a universe from expanding forever.

oscillation model The idea that the universe alternates between phases of expansion and contraction.

pantheist Someone who views the universe itself as some kind of divine being.

paradox Two seemingly contradictory statements or propositions which, once resolved, explain or reveal a more fundamental truth.

peptide bond The linking of a carboxyl group from one amino acid to an amino group of another acid with the resultant release of a water molecule.

perfect cosmological principle The assumption that the mean density of matter in the universe is constant.

photon The smallest unit of light energy capable of existing independently.

Planck time The moment 10^{-43} seconds after the big bang creation event. For any time before this moment, gravity affects *all* physical processes.

presuppositionalism Belief that the existence of God and the authority of the Bible follow from a set of self-evident propositions; and thus, a belief that it is both wrong and useless to appeal to reason and evidence in seeking to win people to Christ.

primeval atom A single, gigantic atom which, as it disintegrated, became the present universe.

protogalaxy A galaxy in its formative stages of development.

proton A positively charged elementary particle with a large mass, also one of the baryons.

protostar A star in its formative stages.

pulsar The collapsed core that remains from a supernova explosion. A pulsar rotates so rapidly (typically about once a second) that energy associated its magnetic field bursts forth once every rotation period.

quantum gravity Physical theories now being designed to cope with conditions before the universe was 10^{-43} seconds old. At 10^{-43} seconds, the force of gravity within the universe becomes comparable to the strong nuclear force. At such a magnitude, gravity may be modified by quantum mechanical effects.

quantum mechanics The realm of micro phenomena in which energy is not infinitely divisible and the micro phenomena possess both wave and particle characteristics.

quantum tunneling The process by which quantum particles penetrate barriers that are insurmountable to classical objects.

quasars The most powerfully radiant objects in the universe, typically emitting more energy than a thousand normal galaxies from a volume only one trillionth that of a normal galaxy.

reconstructionism A doctrinal system combining Puritan beliefs about law, politics, and biblical end-time events with the beliefs of presuppositionalism.

redshift (doppler) A shifting of the spectral lines of a radiating body toward longer wavelengths in direct proportion to the velocity at which that body moves away from the observer.

redshift (gravitational) A shifting of the spectral lines of a radiating body toward longer wavelengths caused, in this case, by the gravitational field of that body.

relativity (general) An extension of special relativity theory to include the effects of gravity on matter, energy, space, and time.

relativity (special) A physical theory derived from the combined propositions that 1) there is no observable absolute motion, only relative motion, and 2) the velocity of light is constant and independent of the motion of the source.

ribosome An organic particle, composed of RNA and certain proteins, used by cells to manufacture other proteins.

ribonucleic acid (RNA) A molecule composed of long chains of phosphate and sugar ribose along with several bases. One form is used by the cell to transfer information from DNA for assembling proteins.

runaway freezing   The cycle which begins when cooler temperatures result in increased snow and ice which in turn cause more sunlight to reflect away from a planet's surface, further lowering the temperature and causing still more snow and ice to form, etc. until the whole surface is frozen.

single revelation theology   The belief that God reveals Himself reliably only through scripture.

singularity   An infinitely shrunken space representing the boundary at which space ceases to exist or at which space comes into existence.

space-time manifold   The four-dimensional continuum of space and time in which all the physical realities of the universe exist.

special creation   The doctrine that God personally intervened in the natural order to produce things that did not previously exist and that could not be produced by natural processes alone.

special revelation   God's expression of Himself to man through the words He inspired certain individuals to write, now collected in one book, the Bible.

specific entropy   The amount of photon entropy per individual proton, an amount which approximately equals the ratio of photons to baryons.

steady state model   The hypothesis that the universe, though expanding indefinitely, takes on an unchanging and eternal quality since the voids that result from expansion are filled by the continual spontaneous generation of new matter.

stellar evolution   The processes by which stars condense out of primordial clouds, ignite nuclear burning processes, exhaust their nuclear fuel, and end their existence either in some kind of explosion or as a slowly dying cinder.

strings   Tubelike configurations of energy that may have formed 10^{-34} seconds after the creation of the universe and may have subsequently served as the condensation centers for galaxy formation.

supernova   The cataclysmic explosion of a massive star in which most of the star is blown off into interstellar space.

theist   Someone who believes that a divine being not only exists but also reveals Himself as the creator and ruler of the universe.

transcendent Existing beyond and apart from the limits of the material universe.

uncertainty principle The principle first stated by Werner Heisenberg that the uncertainty in the *position* of a particle multiplied by the uncertainty in the *velocity* of that particle must be greater than a specified number.

Ussher's chronology A hypothesized calendar of Biblical events based on the assumption that no generations were omitted from the genealogies and that the numbered days of the Genesis creation account were consecutive 24-hour periods.

virial theorem A theorem (applicable to point sources) that enables one to calculate either the dispersal time for star clusters whose total mass is insufficiently condensed for gravitational containment or the time required for the stars of more condensed clusters to assume randomized velocities.

virtual particle A particle created and destroyed in so short a time that violations of energy conservation (in its creation) cannot be detected.

wavelength For any kind of wave, the distance between the peaks (or crests) of successive waves.

young stellar object A large aggregation of gas, dust, and other materials in the process of condensing to become a star.

Name Index

Subject Index

about the author

Hugh Ross earned a B.Sc. in
physics from the University of
British Columbia and an M.Sc.
and Ph.D. in astronomy from
the University of Toronto. For
several years he continued his
research on quasars and galaxies
as a post-doctoral fellow at the
California Institute of Technolo-
gy. For eleven years he served
as minister of evangelism at Sierra Madre Congregational
Church. Today he directs the efforts of Reasons To Believe, an institute founded to research and proclaim the
factual basis for faith in God and in His word, the Bible.
Over the years Hugh has given several hundred lectures,
seminars, and courses, both in America and abroad, on
Christian apologetics. He lives in Southern California with
his wife, Kathy, and sons, Joel and David.

about REASONS TO BELIEVE

REASONS TO BELIEVE is a nonprofit corporation, without
denominational affiliation, adhering to the doctrinal
statements of the National Association of Evangelicals and
of the International Council on Biblical Inerrancy. Its
faculty provide research and teaching on the harmony of
God's dual revelation in the words of the Bible and in the
facts of nature. A catalog of materials on subjects
pertaining to faith, science, and the Bible may be
obtained by phoning (818) 355-6058 or by writing
REASONS TO BELIEVE, P. O. Box 5978, Pasadena, CA 91117.